To Denise and Nick
merry Christmas
and zillions of love
from Chris + Wendy + Joe

PATRICK BARLOW

ALL
THE WORLD'S
A GLOBE

OR

FROM LEMUR TO COSMONAUT
A CONCISE HISTORY OF THE HUMAN RACE

From the Earliest times to 1987

BY

DESMOND OLIVIER DINGLE

With Illustrations by the Author

METHUEN

FOR LUCIA

Designed by Katy Hepburn

First published in Great Britain in 1987
by Methuen London Ltd
11 New Fetter Lane London EC4P 4EE

Copyright © 1987 Patrick Barlow

British Library Cataloguing in Publication Data
Barlow, Patrick
Desmond Oliver Dingle's All the world's
a globe, or, From lemur to cosmonaut: a
concise history of the human race from
the earliest times to 1987.
1. World history – Anecdotes, facetiae,
satire, etc.
I. Title
902'.07   D23.5
ISBN 0-413-35970-4

Made and printed in Great Britain
by R. J. Acford, Chichester, West Sussex

Photoset in Linotron Bembo by
Rowland Phototypesetting Ltd,
Bury St Edmunds, Suffolk

OTHER WORKS⋆
BY
DESMOND OLIVIER DINGLE

So You Want To Act?
A Guide to Sex
'Doreen' – Early verse
The Alexander Technique Explained
Desmond Dingle's I Ching
'All The World's A Globe' for the Young
'All The World's A Globe' for the Elderly
'All The World's A Globe' – Pop-Up Version
Amazing Secrets of the Mystic East
Desmond Dingle's Diaries
Desmond Dingle's Encyclopedia of World
Knowledge (Twelve volumes)
Pamphlets: Was Charles I an Arab?

⋆ *All the above soon to be published by Methuen Books Ltd.*

FOREWORD
by
OMAR SHARIF

Omar Sharif,
Paris.

13 September 1986

Dear Mr Dingle,
   Yes, I did receive the third manuscript of your academic oeuvre 'All the World's a Globe – From Lemur to Cosmonaut'.
   It looks very interesting.
   I will certainly do my best to read it before Christmas, but of course I cannot promise anything.

Yours sincerely

Omar Sharif

Omar Sharif

P.S. Please get off my back.

The author and the publishers are grateful to Sarah Ainslie and Barnaby's Picture Library for permission to reproduce the photographs for 'History in the Home'. Every effort has been made to trace the copyright holders for illustrations and text material quoted, and to make correct acknowledgements. Apologies are made for any errors or omissions.

CONTENTS

CONTENTS

LIST OF PLATES

PREFACE

THE history of the human race is one of the most fascinating stories the world has ever known. Who, surely, could have thought back in the petrified rain forests where now stand modern cities such as Manchester and Nottingham that all the numerous monkeys and lemurs hanging by their tails would one day become Scott of the Antarctic or Madame Pompidou. Surely not even a major historian such as A. P. J. Taylor, when he was a lemur, could have foretold such a future.

In the same fascinating and yet remarkable way, my own career has bloomed with uncanny similarity.

For I too – like a shooting star – have leapt from humble origins to stardom.

Indeed it is almost, in fact, as if I, Desmond Dingle, AM MANKIND ITSELF.

For who could have thought that one day I would become not only famous in the theatrical world but also an authority on the number of things I am now an authority on. Many of which are too numerous to mention at this juncture.

It is a well-known fact, of course, that I begun the National Theatre of Brent from nothing and have made it – without wishing to blow my own trumpet, obviously – into one of our most deeply respected ensemble companies. It is also known that I am a historical expert and a psychotherapist. But what far fewer people know is that I am also a major literary expert as well, which I had in fact been hiding under my bushel until it was 'spotted', as it were, by Sir Geoffrey Methuen who is, as is well known, without doubt the greatest publisher the world has ever known.

In fact, he immediately commanded Methuen's to commission this work shortly before going into a very attractive publishers' retirement bungalow in Bournemouth, where he now resides and from where he has taken a deeply personal interest in the progress of this book.

And so it is with profound gratitude and the deepest humility that I dedicate this *Oeuvre* to Sir Geoffrey Methuen, who 'saw within me a flame no other man could see'.

I can now state that he will not be disappointed.

Desmond Olivier Dingle
Dollis Hill 1987

DEDICATED
TO MY MOTHER
MRS EVADNE DINGLE

SECOND PREFACE

WHEN I was a small boy, lying under the open window above my bedhead, there was nothing I liked more than to hear stories told to me by my father. He would come in and sit down on my blue striped blanket I remember, and I would say to him: 'Please tell me a story.' And he would look down at me and say, 'I will tell you the mighty tales of worlds gone by.'

And as I lay listening, I dreamt that one day, when I too became a man and took up manly pursuits and he was long gone (which he has been now for quite a time, as it happens, seeing as he went on a long journey from whence he did not return) that I might tell those tales again to new generations beneath the same stars.

And so it is that I have been graced with just that privilege, given to me by probably, in my opinion, the greatest publishing house that stands on the Earth.

I humbly thank them and take up my pen. And bend myself before this mighty task to tell the history of the whole Universe from before it was begun to the present. So sit back now and see unfold before you the days gone by until today, so that we may truly understand tomorrow.

Thank you.

Desmond Olivier Dingle
Dollis Hill, 1987

THIRD PREFACE

FINALLY, I should just like to acknowledge my gratitude to Mrs Doreen Wheatley for the kind loan of her felt-tips and, in conclusion, the entire acting company of the National Theatre of Brent – Wallace – for his unstinting support and comments.

Desmond Olivier Dingle
Dollis Hill, 1987

'There's no tomorrow to a willing mind.'
(Lady Winchelsea)

CHAPTER I
THE CREATION OF THE UNIVERSE

'In the beginning was the word.'

(W. Shakespeare)

ORIGINALLY there was nothing, obviously.
And then, one day, there was a very big bang and the sky filled with heavenly bodies and rapidly became very much as it is today.

This is known as the Big Bang Theory and, although nobody knows exactly what the Big Bang Theory is, I believe – along with many numerous other world famous historians – that, all in all, it offers a pretty cogent explanation of how the Universe began.

The Big Bang Theory (also known as the Theory of Relativity[1] or Quantum Theory) was, of course, discovered by Albert Einstein, the celebrated organist, missionary and director of *Battleship Potemkin*. He discovered that, although heavenly bodies generally look very still (unless they're a comet, of course, e.g. Hayley's Comet[2]), because of the Big Bang Theory, they, in fact, aren't. In fact, believe it or not, heavenly bodies are moving through the Universe at unbelievable speeds and often in the opposite direction. As well as also revolving incredibly fast as well, it goes without saying.[3]

---

[1] Also discovered by Charles Dickens of course, in Australia.

[2] Named after Hayley Mills, daughter of Sir John Mills, one of the greatest British actors in the whole world and a close friend of Omar Sharif, the world-famous actor.

[3] This is not the case for our own Sun, Moon and Earth, fortunately, which are all stationary, which is a bit of luck for us, otherwise living a normal life would be virtually impossible.

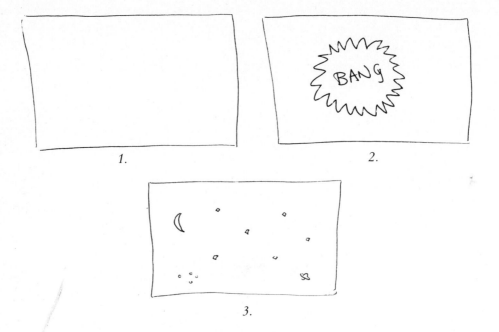

An Illustrated History of the Universe

THINGS TO DO:

1. Visit the world-famous Planetarium in London's Marylebone Road. This is next door to Madame Tussauds. Then visit Madame Tussauds as well, seeing as you get in cheaper if you're already going to the Planetarium. If you are not from London, visit your local planetarium and waxworks, which are traditionally always in the same building.

2. Make a scale model of the Big Bang.

CHAPTER II
THE CREATION OF THE EARTH

'This sceptered orb.'

(W. Shakespeare)

AND so it was that a very big heavenly body appeared[1] in the as yet unformed sky and overlooked what is now the Earth, although it wasn't the Earth then, obviously.

And thus it stood, newly writ upon Heaven's mighty bosoms, until one day – suddenly and without warning – something remarkable occurred. The flaming heavenly body that one day would be named the Sun by a species long since heretofore as yet undreamt of, of whom we ourselves are the inheritors, had a massive but unexpected nocturnal emission. Probably the first in the entire history of the World.

For why, we know not.

Upon what purpose, who could have foreseen?

But from deep within its fiery mantle there shot forth a little tiny gaseous new-born evaporable nomad. A deeply flatulent orb, volatized and aerifying, always on the brink of vanishing totally, yet containing, albeit unknown to itself, those seeds from whence all things would come that is or has been upon the Earth and will be upon the Earth also, in a manner of speaking.

And thus, without wishing to encumber the lay-reader with any more scientific data at this juncture, was the Earth created.[2]

---

[1] Due to the Big Bang Theory. See Chapter I, page 1, ll. 1 onwards.

[2] And then the Moon which shot out of the Earth in more or less the same way, a few years later. Probably, it is now believed, from Northampton.

THINGS TO DO:

1. Paint a mural entitled 'The Creation of the Earth'.

2. Write an Essay entitled: 'How I would create the Earth if I was doing it.'

3. Create the Earth.

CHAPTER III
THE VOLCANIC AGE
A geological history of the Earth

'This burnished ball.'

(D. Dingle)

AFTER a few years, the Earth had numerous earthquakes, volcanoes, continental rifts and mountains which went up and down all the time, until it looked more or less as it looks today, except for the seas which wasn't there, seeing as it hadn't rained yet.

For this reason, there were very few people at this juncture.

THINGS TO DO:

1. Make a scale model of the Himalayas, going up and down.

2. Begin your own collection of rock specimens. There are three basic kinds of rock. Sandstone, from which we get sand; chalk from which we get chalk; limestone from which we get limes and ignatious, named after Ignatious Loyola, the famous loyalist, which serves no purpose.

3. Swap them with your friends.

The Creation of the Midlands 17,000,000,000,000,000 B.C.

CHAPTER IV
THE AGE OF THE EARTH

'Age cannot wither her nor staleness customize her variable infinity.'

(W. Shakespeare)

THERE are, of course, many theories of how old the Earth is. Almost as many theories, probably, as there are grains of sand in all the deserts there have ever been in the whole world put together, I shouldn't wonder.

The ancient Hittites, for instance, believed we was created on 9th February 252 B.C.

Such charmingly naïve notions have now been disproved, of course, by numerous modern world-famous historians like A. P. J. Taylor, Magnus Magnusson and Sir Hugh Trevor Roper (Lord Acton), and by the advent of science, which the Hittites didn't have, obviously, and has really only come in over the last few years. Owing to miraculous scientific and electronic breakthroughs in such things as computer dating, it is now possible to categorically prove that the Earth has been in existence since at least 252,000 B.C. and probably began on 22nd June.

The Dawn of Man
It has also been electronically proved that mankind – the men and women who are the subject of this work – did not start their momentous journey until much more recently than has been supposed. In fact it is now thought that for many years there was no people on the Earth whatsoever. Just a load of animals, birds and plants. And before them, there wasn't even them! The Earth was simply a little revolting ball of dead mountains. Until it rained for approximately 15,000,000,000,000 years which it did for a number of rather complicated technical reasons, thus starting life[1] off as such.

[1] And weather.

THE AGE OF THE EARTH

THINGS TO DO:

1. Make a scale model of the gaseous cloud of inorganic matter containing the seeds of life.

CHAPTER V
LIFE EMERGES

'Who knows from whence life did first emerge?'

(Anon)

AS is well known, the first life appeared in the seas which now covered the Earth, due to the rain. Except for the hills and mountains which was not covered, seeing as the rain stopped, on account of gravity.[1]

The first life were amoebas, many of which were smaller than the

Early Amoeba (from which all life on earth developed)

human eye could see and thus similar to modern-day germs. Not surprisingly, they soon died out, owing to their size, and were replaced by numerous creatures with neither spines nor vertebrates. These included spineless lug-worms, spineless flesh-eating sea millipedes, bloodsucking spineless sea-slugs and poisonous spineless sea-lice, which can't have made

---

[1] Fortunately for non-swimmers, obviously. Like Wallace, my colleague and assistant, for instance. Although, unlike me, as it happens. I am a naturally strong swimmer with a variety of strokes under my belt and would certainly have had no trouble coping with the aquatic state if the rain had in fact not stopped and we now all lived under water. Non- or poor swimmers like Wallace would simply not have survived. As we note in the Theory of Natural Selectivity, discovered by the celebrated Victorian dramatist, Charles Dickens. Mind you, as Dickens makes all too clear in *Martin Chuzzlewit*, if it had never stopped raining, the Earth would have become too heavy and sunk.

life beneath the ocean wave overly pleasant, to put it mildly, seeing as they was all seventy or eighty foot long and slew each other with their massive tentacles willy-nilly, whenever they felt like it.

Bloodsucking spineless Sea-slug

Fortunately, they all became small again, however, so that fish could grow backbones without fear of being strangled. And thus it was that life emerged from the sea.

The Story of Mankind had truly begun, albeit as a Fish.

THINGS TO DO:

1. Make a scale-model of an amoeba.

2. Visit the Geology, Science and Natural History Museums in the heart of London's West End. I have spent many engaging hours here, studying the origins of life and so forth while Wallace experimented with the automatic doors in the Children's Gallery. Of the three museums, the Geology one is fairly boring, seeing as it's all rocks. However, the Earthquake Simulator is a profound experience of spiritual dimensions. It is also free. (Wallace has also asked me to point out the submarine periscope, the working combine harvester, the Whale Hall and the giant womb.)

CHAPTER VI
THE DAWN OF MAN

'A Man's a man for a'that.'

(Sophocles)

ALREADY we have noted the extraordinary and largely unknown fact that for many years there was no people on the Earth.

But for how long?

When was it that Mankind finally appeared in the primogenital vista?

In order to answer these fascinating questions, let us begin with a simple but daring analogy. And compare the length of time that mankind has walked upon the Earth with the length of time that scientists, such as myself, now believe that the Earth has been here, on its own, without man on it, as it were.

Imagine, therefore, the Earth's history as being the entire length of the M1 motorway, up to, and including, the Leeds underpass at Junction 47. If we was to do this, we would be truly amazed, as indeed I was, to discover that the history of humanity would have started *no sooner* than the round-about at Hunslett,[1] which, of course, is a mere one and a half miles from the City Centre of Leeds itself, which is where, following the allusion through, we – the Human Race – stand today. At the centre of Leeds.

This is not, in fact, entirely accurate, seeing as the motorway does actually stop *before* the City Centre and becomes the A58, which by-passes Leeds and heads off towards Weatherby, where it becomes the A1 to Catterick and Scotch Corner. But nevertheless, modern man *would* be standing in the Centre of Leeds, if the motorway did end there. (A town-planner's nightmare, clearly, which is why it doesn't.)

In other words – if the first spark of life leapt from the heart of the Sun

---

[1] Wallace's mother, apparently, was born near Hunslett.

and created the protoplasmic and bio-energetic cloudlet that became the Earth at Staples Corner,[1] then the ancestors of you and I and Wallace do not even begin the momentous journey that is, of course, the subject of this oeuvre *until Junction 44.*

Or even Junction 45!

And this remarkable and audacious analogy becomes even more unbelievable when we realize that the dinosaurs (popularly relegated to a mere thirty or forty years' worth of evolutionary trial and error) actually began to lumber through the petrified swamps of the prehistoric landscape at around Junction 21. And didn't finally peter out till the Granada Services at Trowell.[2] Twenty-seven miles later!

THINGS TO DO:

1. Don't go driving all over the M1 just to test this theory. Take my word for it. The M1 is crowded enough as it is. Besides which, most of it has collapsed anyway due to overcrowding in the inner cities and nationwide mining subsidence. Despite British Engineering, of course, which is famed throughout the world for such feats as the Clifton Suspension Bridge, the QE2 and the Taj Mahal.

---

[1] For international readers, Staples Corner is a famous Wembley landmark lying at the top of the Edgware Road.

[2] Near Nottingham. One of England's loveliest cities. Home of Britain's thriving lace industry and D. H. Lawrence the celebrated pornographic novelist.

CHAPTER VII
THE BIRTH OF THE DINOSAURS

'Flee fro' the prees.'

(G. Chaucer)

THIS is even more amazing when we recollect that many dinosaurs had brains the size of Brussels sprouts.

And those were the bright ones.

Less fortunate dinosaurs had brains the size of baked beans and took at least six weeks of relentless brain-racking even to turn round. While some of the greatest dinosaurs that ever lived had brains the size of raisins and never *did* turn round. In other words, their brains were so small it took them most of their time just working out how to stay on four legs. Unless, of course, they had two legs, which took even longer.

For the dinosaur, eating, for instance, became a massively complex process and a simple two- or three-course dinner could take months from start to finish. The main problem with eating for the dinosaur was that his brain – being so pathetically minuscule – had no room in it for what we in the medical profession call 'Memory Retention'. In other words, not only did the dinosaur have extreme difficulty in remembering what was food and what wasn't, but also, and more crucial, he was always forgetting what feeling hungry felt like. So that many dinosaurs never actually knew they were hungry and often dropped dead without ever having had a meal.

This – I hope – will once and for all solve the so-called mystery of why the dinosaurs died out. In a nutshell – the dinosaurs died out because they were stupid.

HOW WE KNOW NO. 1

The dinosaurs that did eat tended generally to be either carnivorous or herbaceous and we can tell by their skulls which one they were by examining its teeth. See illustration.

Fig. 1. *Skull of Carnivorous Dinosaur.*

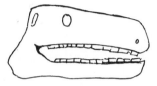

Fig. 2. *Skull of Herbaceous Dinosaur*

(Note: The carnivorous teeth are pointed and the herbaceous flat so as to chew numerous plants with.)

It goes without saying, obviously, that the carnivorous dinosaurs, being meat-eaters, tended to eat the herbaceous dinosaur, seeing as the herbaceous dinosaur (a) couldn't bite the carnivore back because of his flat teeth (b) couldn't turn round anyway (*see* p. 12) and (c) didn't actually want to bite the carnivore because he was a vegetarian with a vegetarian instinct which is basically to find meat repulsive.[1] We can imagine, therefore, the anguish of one such herbaceous dinosaur, his little tail already caught in the vice-like jaws of a Tyrannosaurus and his minuscule brain working overtime, sending contradictory messages up and down his tragically massive body. 'Bite, Bite!' says one. 'You must protect your life.' 'No, No!' says the other. 'Do not bite him. You do not like meat. You are herbaceous. Meat makes you ill. Besides which he is a creature of the earth like you. He is your brother. You love all creatures. You are a vegetarian.'

This raging inner dialogue probably taxed the dinosaur's brain and body to such an extent that it died of a heart attack anyway, which presumably would have been preferable to being hacked to death in a tar swamp by a Tyrannosaurus Rex who's just discovered he's hungry after ninety-five years.

---

[1] I happen to know this, because I myself am a vegetarian and have numerous vegetarian friends and poets, many of whom throw up in a restaurant if they so much as smell meat.

*Two famous dinosaurs. The long-necked Diplodocus (*diplo = *long;* docus = *neck) talks to a Triceratops, the celebrated three-horned dinosaur (*tri = *three;* cera = *horns;* tops = *on the top of his head).*

THINGS TO DO:

1. See the two archaeological films: *One Million Years B.C.* and *When Dinosaurs Ruled The Earth*, starring Raquel Welch.

CHAPTER VIII
THE ADVENT OF
MAMMALS

'Life is a mixture of sunshine and rain,
 Good things and bad things, pleasure and pain,
 We can't all have sunshine, but it's certainly true
 There is never a cloud the sun doesn't shine through.'

(Helen Steiner Rice – *Just for You*)

MAMMALS came after dinosaurs but before man, although man is a mammal seeing as he is born alive and has breasts.

The five chief advantages of being a mammal as opposed to a dinosaur are:–

1. Mammals are furrier.[1]
2. Mammals are smaller. And therefore able to hide easily. For a fifth-century Diplodocus, the length of twelve London buses end to end, finding a suitable hiding place would have been well-nigh impossible. Even if it had a brain the size of a bungalow. Mind you, if it *had* had a brain the size of a bungalow, its neck would have collapsed and it couldn't have moved anywhere anyway. It would have been a phenomenally intelligent vegetable. As opposed to a very stupid vegetable, which is what it was, of course.
3. Dinosaurs are reptiles.

---

[1] Except for man who is devoid of hair generally (apart from certain more masculine men, such as myself, interestingly enough). And elephants. And rhinos. And hippos obviously. And whales. And hedgehogs.

THINGS TO DO: .

1. Make a list of the advantages of being an insect as opposed to a fish.

2. Make a scale model of a mammal.

CHAPTER IX
THE DAWN OF MAN

'This was the noblest Roman of them all;
All the conspirators save only he
Did that they did in envy of great Caesar;
He, only, in a general honest thought
And common good to all, made one of these.
His life was gentle, and the elements
So mixed in him that Nature might stand up
And say to all the world, "This was a Man."'

(Shakespeare)

IT will now be clear to even the most backward student that man didn't just appear from nowhere. In other words, it wasn't all animals and plants one day and then animals and plants and man the next. He didn't just wander out from behind a petrified forest looking like any common or garden man in the street.

No. Man *became* man. In other words, like everything else, he was not a man originally. Originally, he was a lemur. Well, originally, he was a fish, as we noted in the previous chapter. Or rather two fish. Which means that – originally – he was just an amoeba. Which means, of course, to be strictly logical, he was, in fact, a direct result of that very first nocturnal emission. Which means that *originally* he wasn't anything. In other words, and to cut a long story short, *we have all evolved from nothing*, which is a pretty remarkable thought when you think about it.

This, basically, is the famous Theory of Evolution (or Gravity) which was of course discovered by Charles Darwin, the celebrated Australian novelist already mentioned, who also discovered Relativity, jet propulsion and New Zealand, and spent most of his life on the famed 'Lost Island' of Galapagos near Tahiti, after the Mutiny on the Bounty, where he bred giant tortoises and massive vegetables and became enamoured of a scantily clad native girl.[1]

As is well known, he was tortured by the Church of England for his beliefs until he recanted and left for Florence. Nevertheless, old, bitter and blind he went on working in secret and smuggled his master work inside a stuffed goose into the hands of the Curator of Melbourne Zoo shortly before his death from massive vegetable poisoning in 1871.

His name is remembered throughout Australia in such places as Darwin, Port Darwin, Darwin River, Little Darwin, Greater Darwin, Darwin-on-Tees and Wagga Wagga.[2]

The Discovery of Australia and New Zealand by Thomas Cooke

THINGS TO DO:

1. Write an essay entitled 'Australia and New Zealand – a Paradise on Earth.'

[1] The subject of famed bearded novelist William Golding's celebrated novel *Lord of the Rings*.

[2] At this point I would just like to take this opportunity of introducing myself, and my trainee Wallace, to any new Australian friends we might be making as a result of their possibly reading this volume, hopefully. And I would just like to say – on behalf of both of us – that I have, in fact, had the enormous privilege of meeting a number of Australian people in my life, all of whom I have found very interesting in every aspect. I have also met a number of New Zealand people as well and they have all been very nice too. In fact Australians and New Zealanders are, in my opinion, *certainly the most delightful people I have met in my entire life*. If, by any chance, any Australians or New Zealanders would like to know if Wallace or myself might be interested in a cultural lecture tour of Australia and New Zealand, and Bali possibly, and maybe even Japan, China, Hong Kong and the South Pacific, then I would just like to say that if such an offer were forthcoming we would almost certainly be guaranteed to be available and interested; or if not Wallace, certainly I would, for a reasonable fee, obviously, at relatively short notice. Please contact Methuen Books, or if they're closed, me personally.

POPULAR MISCONCEPTIONS NO. 1

Life emerged from the sea. This is true. But it is certainly not true that animals, birds and plants etc. just trooped out on to the beach in the perfectly formed state in which we know them today. All these creatures, in fact, evolved from two prehistoric fish who are now extinct but who came out of the water first. They were called Eusthenopteron and took the decision on behalf of all living things that would ever be, apart from modern-day fish obviously, that the land had more going for it than the sea.

However grateful we may now be that they did decide to leave their ocean home, the Eusthenopteron (from *eus* = very hard, *then* = to walk, *opt* = let alone, *eron* = to breathe) must have had a rather warped

False

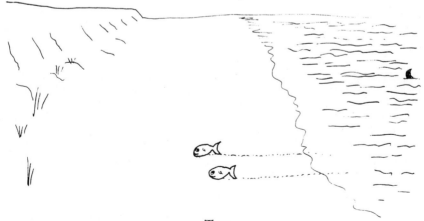

True

perspective on things, if we consider the alternatives that must have faced them in that crucial turning point in the history of the world.

For a strange choice it must have been to turn your back on a pleasant warm ocean bed, with little coral reefs and rocky coves, endless forms of seaweed and a massive supply of trilobites and plankton, to heave out on to the sand, beneath a burning sun, and start hacking out, *on fins*, into a landscape that would have made Death Valley look like Disneyland. With no prospects whatsoever apart from finishing up on some crag as a pterodactyl's regurgitated pudding.

In other words, mankind's historic transition from water to land was, in all probability, the result of an act of psychotic lunacy.

CHAPTER X
MAN AFTER HE WAS A LEMUR

'So what come of man
After he was a lemur?' (Milton)

L ET us now return to the evolutionary journey of man after he was a
lemur. Obviously he didn't become a man straight after being a lemur.
In order to facilitate becoming a man he became an ape first, which
obviously looks a lot more similar to a man than a lemur. In other words,
you'd never look at a lemur and say: 'There's a little rudimentary man.' In
fact there are no similarities whatsoever to the naked eye.

LITTLE-KNOWN FACTS NO. 1

This is the fossil of a dinosaur dropping. It is the size of Wembley
Stadium and is called a *coprolite* (from *copra* = a large amount of unpleasant
non-essential matter and *lite* = that which is dropped from a great height).
The study of *coprolites* is called *coprology* and is carried out by *coprologists*
who often devote their entire lives to the study of these great and terrible
artefacts.

Coprologists have few friends and generally live alone.

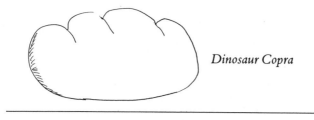

Dinosaur Copra

21

Anyway, having been a lemur, and then an ape, man finally became a man. Which is what we are today, obviously. Unless we're a woman, of course. Which many of us are as well. Fortunately for the Human Race, if I may say so! Naturally, those early humans or 'homo erectus' as they became known would have been a very far cry from you or me in terms of looks. Hardly Michelangelo's David,[1] in other words.

Michelangelo's David (artist's reconstruction)

Or Omar Sharif,[2] if you get my meaning. Not, of course, that we can all claim to look like Omar Sharif or Michelangelo's David. Some of us, obviously, but not everybody. I, for instance have been blessed with rather above average looks, I'm happy to say (*see* front cover) – a feature noted by a number of people, particularly certain members of the fairer sex as it happens. But even those less physically appealing than myself (like Wallace, for instance) would have looked positively mouth-watering in comparison with those early hominids, lumbering through the primordial rain forests with great hairy bodies, pointed foreheads, massive jaws and horribly prehensile thumbs. In other words, although they was in fact humans, they still looked identical to the apes which they had just been before they became human. They was in fact humans trapped in an ape's body. Which must have been an extraordinarily painful experience if you think about it.

So – I hear you ask – if he was, to all intents and purposes, an ape, how come he become a human like we are today?

For one simple, essential and obvious reason.

HE HAD A HUMAN BRAIN.

Where he found it need not concern us. For nobody knows. Suffice it to say he had one. In other words, he was only a great hairy primate *on the outside*. Inside he was as human as you or I. Needless to say, we didn't all

---

[1] The famous statue by Leonardo da Vinci.

[2] The famous stage and screen actor, whose films include *Lawrence of Arabia* and *Doctor Zhivago*, to name but a few. Along with Sir Laurence Olivier and Charlton Heston, Omar Sharif is probably the greatest actor of this century.

turn overnight into Miriam Stoppard, probably one of the most intelligent people in the world and one of the most charming too, if I may say so. Not that I have had the pleasure of meeting her personally, but judging by her very warm television manner that has endeared her to millions. In other words, brains weren't always what they are now. And the early human brain – while being massively more advanced than apes' or dinosaurs' brains, with a host of new features – was certainly not the intricate piece of equipment we walk around with nowadays.

The Development of the Brain

The *earliest* human brain was approximately the equivalent size and, in some respects, texture of a King Edward potato. Its main advantage over dinosaurs' and apes' brains being that while dinosaurs' and apes' brains gave them rudimentary skills such as walking, eating and going to the toilet, they didn't give them the essential brainal requisites of knowing *when* or *where* to do these things. To go to the toilet for example.

TEACHERS

PLEASE NOTE THIS PAGE CARRIES SOME EX-PLICIT BIOLOGICAL DETAIL AND MAY NOT BE APPROPRIATE FOR YOUNGER CHILDREN.

The Dinosaur's raisin-sized brain, for instance, would just go to the toilet anywhere, regardless of time and place, and must have been most unpleasant – particularly seeing as dinosaurs' bladders were often the size of three cricket pitches end to end, and, worse, their 'bowel disposal equipment', as it is known geologically, would often pass non-essential food-matter or *copras* (*see* 'Little Known Facts' p. 21) equivalent to the size of seven First World War Zeppelins.

Anyway, the brains expanded and developed, and developed gradually more and more features until the current modern-day brain appeared which controls not only the complete human orgasm but is also capable of a staggering number of capabilities, many of which we don't know we have, like bending forks, turning tennis balls inside out, flying in our astral bodies and E.S.N. In fact, the modern-day brain is now so well developed that if it got any bigger it would burst through our heads and we would probably die of brain exposure.

And so it was the advent of the human brain that gave man the revolutionary idea of standing on two legs, thus setting him apart, once and for all, from every other living creature on the planet, all of whom have four feet. (Except for kangaroos and fish.)[1]

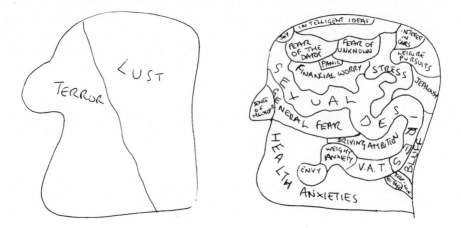

Comparison of the brains of Prehistoric and Modern Man

THINGS TO DO:

1. Make a scale model of a lemur turning into an ape.

2. Dissect a lemur brain.

3. Write an essay entitled: 'Copras – discuss.'

[1] And millipedes, centipedes, flies, bluebottles, birds, octopuses, spiders, jellyfish, seagulls, prawns and snakes. Thank you, Wallace.

CHAPTER XI

THE EMERGENCE OF CIVILIZATION

'Civilization gradually emerged.' (D. Dingle)

A ND so – at last – Civilization began to emerge. As rudimentary men and women – with their ever-complicating brains and rapidly moulting bodies – began to venture across the shifting continents of the Earth on their endless quest for some of those things that we, now, of course, take so much for granted – fire,[1] water, sheep, nuts, paint, God, mammoths, to name but a few.

[1] I wish I was able to recommend the foreign film *Quest for Fire*, but I'm afraid it left a considerable amount to be desired. The scenery and costumes were very poor, there was no dinosaurs and only one mammoth. But what really took the biscuit was the screenplay for which Anthony Burgess the famous novelist (*The Clockwork Orange*, *The Magnus*, *The White Hotel*, *The Guns of Navarone*) was credited. Believe it or not, in a full-length feature film for family audiences, there was *not a single word spoken*. Just grunting! For two and a half hours! *And not only that.* Desmond Morris, the eminent psychiatrist and compère of *Zoo Time* was credited as Movement Coach! Which would have been all very well except that all they did was jump up and down and do a number of revolting and explicit things in caves which I'm quite sure even rudimentary men and women would never have got up to even if they *were* in the middle of evolving. If I'd have been the film company, I'd have sued them both! Next time they might care to watch a *real* film on the subject with proper costumes, music and scenery. And words! *When Dinosaurs Ruled The Earth*, for instance. They might then get a couple of famous faces to appear perhaps. I noticed that the artists I would have personally approached – Omar Sharif, Charlton Heston, Sir Alec Guinness, Dame Peggy Ashcroft, Helen Mirren – gave the film a *very* wide berth. Readers may be interested to note that I have in fact written my own rather more realistic Stone-Age filmscript: *Quest for Berries* which deals with the plight of a Stone-Age vegetarian girl living in a carnivorous world of primitive lust and greed. On her quest she meets a Stone-Age hermit man with extraordinary telepathic powers, and falls in love with a Stone-Age Egyptian warrior who has just invented the wheel. Together they bring peace to the whole Earth.

I say 'shifting', not as a passing comment on man's fickle territorial habits and ever-changing alliances (which well I might if I was commenting on the behavioural patterns of modern humankind), but because the planetary land masses was still banging and shifting about and changing places and generally re-aligning themselves all over the place. Still deciding, as it were, on how finally to form themselves when they finally stopped shifting. In other words – even as those first heroic rudimentary men and women were taking their first tentative steps upon *terra firma* – Africa was still joined to North America, Australia was part of Holland, China was bashing against Scotland, and Norway was still an indiscriminate lump on the edge of Peru. In other words, *terra firma* was not very firm at all, basically.

However, there were benefits. For many years, for instance, and not many people know this, *there was no English Channel* joining Great Britain to the Continent. So that a day trip to France, for instance, would simply have been a question of walking. Which must have come as a welcome relief on a journey otherwise fraught with woolly rhinos, cave painting smugglers, disused mammoth traps and volcanoes. Unfortunately, however, because of the planetary shifting, no land mass could ever be relied upon to stay in the same place for any guaranteed length of time. Thus one of the greatest terrors of the epoch was what scientists now call *Land Disappearance*. Many was the time, in other words, that a troupe of cavemen would reappear after a week-end in Calais or Dieppe, with their baguettes and bucket of hot coals, only to find that Britain had totally disappeared and was in fact at that moment nuzzling up to Spain, nine thousand miles away.

Land Replacement, on the other hand, was an even more heart-rending problem. When you'd wake up one morning and find yourself floating past Tibet. These were difficult and rudimentary times.[1] The only thing there was no shortage of at this time was, in fact, stones, which were everywhere. Hence the title of this age which was known as the Stone Age – as it is to this day. Naturally, although Civilization was definitely emerging at this time – as I have already stated – it couldn't *completely* emerge until the Stone Age, which was very uncivilized, had actually finished. Which it did quite soon, fortunately, seeing as it only lasted ten or eleven years.

The correct technical or archaeological term for Stone-Age people was *cavemen*, seeing as they lived in caves. Which are generally found in rural areas such as the Peak District.[2] Cavemen and Cavewomen decorated their

---

[1] To put it mildly.

[2] Note to overseas readers, particularly from Australia, New Zealand and Canada: the Peak District is an attractive beauty-spot in England's Derbyshire. Possibly it could be described as a rather gentle version of the Rockies or the Barrier Reef. If you ever fancy a week-end away in the Peak District or any of our lovely beauty-spots, please don't hesitate

caves with cave paintings although, unfortunately, they were appallingly unlifelike and crude.

THINGS TO DO:

1. Construct a Stone-Age lunar observatory.

2. Visit a Stone-Age ruin.

3. Discuss Civilization generally.

---

to get in touch with the English Tourist Board or, directly, with Holidays and Tourist Enquiries, c/o Methuen Books Ltd., New Fetter Lane, London E.C.1, who will be most happy to advise on trips, accommodation, suggested clothing, bargain fares etc.

CHAPTER XII

THE IRON AGE

'This, truly, is an iron Age!'

(Anon)

AFTER the Stone Age was the Iron Age which also came just before the gradual emergence of Civilization and was very interesting.

The Iron Age was famous for Stonehenge which came from Wales by boat.

Famous Iron-Age queens was Boadicea, and everything was made of iron generally.

THINGS TO DO:

1. Find out more about the Iron Age.

Queen Boadicea (Iron-Age ancestor of our own Queen)

CHAPTER XIII
THE BRONZE AGE

'All that glistens is not bronze.'

(W. Shakespeare)

THE Bronze Age also came before the gradual emergence of Civilization and was also very interesting.

THINGS TO DO:

1. Make a Bronze-Age hat.

CHAPTER XIV
THE EGYPTIANS

'We are all in the gutter but some of us are looking at the stars.'

(Oscar Wilde)

IT was then that Civilization emerged with a number of very famous ancient Civilizations. One of the most famous ancient Civilizations was the Egyptians', whom I find personally a very interesting people, not least because of their interest in re-incarnation, which I have personally experienced, as it happens (*see below*).

The Sphinx (now extinct)

Besides building the pyramids (*see below*) and doing the Sphinx (*see above*), the Egyptians built Cairo, Abu Simbel and became renowned for their wall-paintings, which aren't overly lifelike, to put it mildly. In fact they had no idea of perspective whatsoever (like Turner or Constable), but then again nobody did at that time.

The Egyptians were an exotic people, who wore a form of kilt and mitre generally, and spent much of their time feasting, dancing, hunting hippo and keeping their slaves in bondage. They was also famous for embalming their ancestors, cats, dogs and numerous other people. Naturally it was the Pharaohs (similar to our Queen) and the priests (Mrs Thatcher, Norman Tebbit etc.) who done the hippo hunting and the embalming. The working-class people and the enslaved nations, like the

Israelites, who was the most famous and wrote the Old Testament, lived in windowless holes in the ground and spent their entire lives making twenty-ton bricks for the pyramids (*see below*). Their hobbies were few and far between and they certainly had no time for feasting or dancing or hunting anything. In fact the closest they got to any wild life was the Pharaoh's crocodiles, to whom they were fed periodically, either as a warning, as a mystic ceremony, or just anyway. Some slaves indulged in illicit flamingo-baiting but the bodily positions into which the culprits were embalmed as their punishment were so horrifying and embarrassing that only the most foolhardy continued in this illegal practice.

When the Pharaoh died, he was, of course, embalmed himself, along with three or four hundred hand-picked slaves, who was embalmed with him. He was then called a Mummy. Being a hand-picked embalmed slave was obviously a much sought-after position and definitely preferable to making bricks in a four-foot windowless hole in the Nile Delta. For this reason, slaves had their names on the Local Embalmment List from an early age. At the time of a Pharaoh's death, Cairo was always packed with young hopefuls hoping to be spotted in the souks and smoky bars and plucked from papyrus-grinding obscurity into a life of eternal embalmment. Interest in embalmment fell off dramatically in the sixth century, however, when it was discovered that embalmment entailed being killed first.

Re-Incarnation

The Egyptians believed in re-incarnation which is a theory, popular today, that we have all lived before in another time and endlessly live again, going round and round and being different people and animals and so forth till we become totally enlightened and have no need to live on the earth no more.

I have researched this subject quite considerably with numerous experts under hypnotic regression, and I can now reveal that I *myself* was Rameses II, the scourge of the Israelites, for which I am, of course, very sorry, and would like to make it quite clear that I will never do anything like that again, and was played by Yul Brynner in *The Ten Commandments*, which is one of the greatest films ever made, as is well known. I also have evidence that I was Alfred the Great, Gandhi, Robin Hood, Abraham Lincoln, Joan of Arc and Freud. Some of this evidence has come about through hypnosis and some through inexplicable bodily sensations. For instance, I now have incontrovertible evidence that I am in fact the reincarnated spirit of Pablo Picasso, the world famous modern painter who died in 1973, as I have recently begun to feel strange psychic tremors in Spanish restaurants and a driving inner compulsion to paint cubes. I have also undergone experiments in which I have had tantalizing glimpses of past lives which *I haven't yet had*. These include a Hollywood teen idol, two world leaders, a Pope, a Captain of the English cricket team, a fabulously wealthy heart specialist and a member of the Royal Family (probably

King).[1] The Egyptians worshipped many gods, as we all do to this day. Many of them with the heads of dogs and cats, rabbits and owls. They was also famous for Antony and Cleopatra and the Suez Canal.

A final note

One of the great tragedies in the film world is that Omar Sharif has never acted in a film about ancient Egypt. This is particularly sad seeing as Mr Sharif is actually Egyptian and therefore would be ideal casting. May I suggest that the next time an ancient Egyptian film comes up he should be immediately contacted before it's too late!

And thus it was that the Sun set on the mighty Egyptian Empire.

THINGS TO DO:

1. Draw the inside of a slave's hovel.

2. Embalm a dead creature.

3. Design a tomb for a friend.

POPULAR MISCONCEPTIONS NO. 2

The Pyramids

These were first discovered by Lord Carter of Caernarvon, the famous Welsh archaeologist. Resulting, of course, in the immediate death of himself and his heirs, owing to the celebrated curse left there by the Pharaohs for such an eventuality and from which his family are still perishing to this day.

I, along with many other poets and famous archaeologists, have marvelled at these mysterious edifi, standing like silent sentinels, witnesses to the cruel passing of time. I, too, have paced the sands wondering what purpose these buildings served and to what strange use they were put by that people about whom we know all too little. Finally I reached the conclusion that each pyramid was in fact the *roof* of some form of regal dwelling-house. A country retreat, perhaps, or an ancient Chequers, where the Pharaoh and her cabinet could quietly order their governmental tasks, far from the hurly-burly of noisesome plague-infested Cairo. A

---

[1] In similar experiments that I have conducted with Wallace, we have discovered that his future past lives will include a train-driver, a rabbit, a library attendant, another train-driver and a geranium. All exciting in their way, obviously, though not quite as spectacular as mine, it goes without saying. I mention this not to idly compare my rather more glorious future with Wallace's, although it does look like it will be, but simply to show how important it is to remember how we are all different and yet the same in many respects, which is very important to remember in my opinion.

regal dwelling that had sunk inch by inch over the centuries into the shifting desert sands (which, of course, make up a large proportion of the Egyptian terrain), leaving only the massive stone-built roof remaining to public gaze.

However, I should now like to make known an extraordinary discovery that has recently come to my attention. Namely that there is, in fact, *nothing* below these imposing monuments. They are simply standing on *top* of the sand. And were probably used, according to certain evidence that has only just come into my possession, as TOMBS. *To put the Pharaohs in.* Once they'd been embalmed, obviously. Along with three hundred slaves, numerous horses, kitchen goods and various household gadgets.

To be perfectly honest, I always felt the old Roof Theory to be rather dubious, owing to the fact that the sloping roof was invented for the rainy climate and therefore, if the pyramids *were* roofs, then the fact that they are at least 2,000 feet tall would be massively disproportionate to the fact that rain is a totally unknown quantity in Egypt. Also there are no chimneys, which there would be if it was a roof, obviously.

And thus it was that the Sun set on the mighty Egyptian empire.

THE STORY OF MOSES:
A famous story

One of the most famous stories about the Egyptians was the story of Moses, who was put by his mother in the Nile in a Hebrew linen basket and daubed in river mud so that it would not sink. Pharaoh's daughter happened to be bathing in the Nile on that day and she saw the Hebrew linen basket and did not think anything more of it seeing as people had no concern about river pollution in those days generally and chucked all and sundry in there without a thought. But then it was she heard a baby's cry and quickly bade her serving maid to rescue the basket, which she done.

Pharaoh's daughter had never had children owing to a disorder in her genealogical areas of rather an intimate nature, obviously, that we do not need to go into in a textbook of this nature, which will probably be used by schoolchildren the world over. Thus she found the babe and said:

'He will be mine and I must have a nursemaid to look after him.' Whereupon immediately Moses's sister who had been hiding in the reeds leapt up, and said:

'Oddly enough I am a professional nursemaid, oh Mighty Pharaoh's daughter. I could not help overhearing what you were saying.'

'Very well, Hebrew slave, you will be his nursemaid, but what will I call him?'

'Excuse me, oh Mighty Daughter of the incarnated Sun on Earth, you could call him Moses.'

'Moses?'

'Possibly.'

'But does that not mean: "He who will lead and deliver his people out of bondage, will see God in a burning bush, get the Ten Commandments, be responsible for endless frogs and locusts and boils and the deaths of all the Egyptian first-born, drown the Egyptian armies and Pharaoh personally in the Red Sea and set free all the Israelites so that the Egyptians will have to build the sodding pyramids themselves"?'

'No, it means: "He who was washed up in a laundry basket and found by Pharaoh's daughter".'

'How lovely. In that case I will call him Moses.'

Thus the story goes on. A very beautiful story known throughout the world and filmed – as I have already mentioned – as *The Ten Commandments* starring Charlton Heston and Yul Brynner. Unfortunately, we do not have time in this work to go into the whole of the story of Moses, owing to the fact that it is extremely long.

And thus it was that the Sun set on the mighty Egyptian Empire.

Egyptian Sunrise

CHAPTER XV
THE CHINESE EMPIRE

克ヒ回ㄱ㇇㈐㇇㇂㇇回ㅋ

(Anon)

THE Chinese Empire is one of the oldest Empires in the world and existed until recently without anyone knowing about it. Apart from the Chinese, obviously.

The Chinese People

The Chinese People were generally very down-trodden and ill. They made their living as slaves to the Emperors, for which they were not paid, owing to the fact that they were peasants. They had no say whatsoever in their own government and if anyone *did* say anything they were immediately killed without redress. Hence their reputation, to this day, as a rather unforthcoming people. They generally caught horrible diseases like cholera, yellow fever and smallpox and had no form of heating, lighting, medical treatment or hope. Nevertheless, they amused themselves with rudimentary sports such as ping-pong, darts, conjuring, shadow puppets and a rather adult form of charades, or *Kabuki Theatre*,[1] which was most popular of all. And must account in part for the massive Chinese birthrate which increased daily, despite cholera, wars, famine, plague and death generally.

The Emperors

The Emperors, on the other hand, lived very pleasant lives in large paper-built pagodas and spent most of their time cultivating silkworms, eating lychees and worshipping their ancestors. This was known as Ances-

---

[1] *Kabuki = Ka* – adult; *bu* – form of; *ki* – charades

tor Worship and is based on the belief that as soon as an ancestor dies he becomes a god. This was a very clever circumlocution around the problem, redolent in many societies, that some ancestors want to be gods before they're dead. But the point is you can't *be* an ancestor if you're still alive, obviously. So it was impossible for the ancestors of the Chinese Emperors to become gods until they was completely deceased. Which saved considerable internecine difficulties, not surprisingly.

Dynasties

The Emperors themselves ruled what was known as Dynasties which, generally speaking, lasted about five hundred years before moving on to the next one. The Emperor would rule the Dynasty and the Dynasty would rule the Peasants.

Chinese Political and Economic Infrastructure (Detailed diagram)

Each Dynasty obviously had its own laws, fashions and behavioural modes and most important of all had its own Vase, which as soon as a new Dynasty came in was immediately sent out and copied throughout the land. So, for instance, when the Ming Dynasty came in, everyone had to make Ming vases and send back their previous vases which happened to be Ch'ung vases. These were then smashed up by the government in ancient vase disposal units, similar to our modern-day bottle banks. Some people didn't return their vases but buried them or sent back fakes and then nipped them over the border to sell them as antiques in Japan or Hong Kong. We still find them in antique shops to this day. A Ming vase or Shang vase can fetch a fortune. Vase smuggling was punishable by death, but then that wasn't particularly unusual, seeing as virtually everything was punishable by death.

Ming Vase   *Other Chinese Vases*

The Shang Dynasty
The first Dynasty was the Shang Dynasty who ruled from the earliest times and achieved a high degree of Civilization, while Stone-Age man in Britain was still half an ape, grubbing for wood-lice and eating each other's brains. (This unpleasant Stone-Age habit was not mentioned in previous chapters owing to the fact that I've only just heard about it on a very interesting and intellectual television quiz show that I happen to enjoy watching. Apparently they ate each other's brains to make themselves cleverer. However, it's certainly not something you'd catch me doing, even if I was offered a bowlful of A. P. J. Taylor's brains.) The Shang Dynasty also saw the introduction of soya sauce, noodles and prawn balls.

The Chou Dynasty
The Shang Dynasty became obsessed with Chinese cooking and, although they also invented the wok and discovered sweet and sour pork, they lost the hearts of the man in the street and were finally displaced by the Chou Dynasty, a cruel and heartless race of Anatolian horse salesmen, who swept down from the south and cleaned up within two or three months. They had little interest in cooking, although they did introduce Chinese cabbage, and thus revolutionized the making of coleslaw.

Marco Polo, or Mark Long as he was called in England, discovered Chinese cabbage and introduced it into Europe, particularly France, who was so impressed they decided to use the name of the Great Chinese Dynasty as their word for cabbage.

Chinese wealth – reasons
The massive wealth of China has always rested on its three main staples, rice, bamboo and staples. Rice has a double function and can be used both as a main course and as a dessert, in the form of rice pudding. It can also be turned into rice paper, which is useful for writing secret messages on, and also for making very thin sandwiches. Bamboo is used for cooking, in the form of bamboo shoots that you can have with the rice and also, in its mature form, for gardening (as raspberry canes, holding up tomato plants etc.). Staples are used for joining paper together and were also fed to the peasants in time of famine.

Chinese Houses
China is celebrated for its very bad earthquakes which occur once every few weeks. For this reason, they build their houses from cardboard so that no-one is hurt when the houses fall down, which they do constantly.

The Chinese
The Chinese invented most things, as they do to this day. They invented the Peking Opera, the most famous of which was *The Mikado* by Gilbert

and Sullivan, and also books, written from back to front and from bottom to top for no reason that has yet been discerned.

They also invented banshee wailers, tin-openers, hydro-electricity, Aladdin heaters, kimonos, the take-away meal and acupuncture.[1]

The Chinese people's lot became more and more unbearable under the Dynasties so they had a cultural Revolution which meant everyone wore the same suit and made farm machinery, but was much more cultured as a result.

THINGS TO DO:

1. Write a detailed, diagrammatic analysis of Confucian thought.

2. Make a Chinese hat or useful lampshade (*see diagram below*).

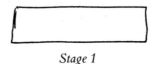

Stage 1

Stage 2

---

[1] The impaling of the body on numerous razor-sharp needles for long periods of time in small rooms in North London. It is renowned throughout the world and used by film stars and royalty alike and also by myself as it happens. In fact I would like to say, at this juncture, that I have personally derived enormous benefit from this form of healing which, despite the intense agony of the process itself, has left me feeling exceptionally balanced and fulfilled on a very deep spiritual level.

CHAPTER XVI
MINOS AND THE CRETANS

*'I wandered lonely as a cloud
that floats on high o'er vales and hills.'*

(Wordsworth)

AFTER the Chinese Empire, the next major empire was Crete who were the cradle of Western Civilization and lived on the island of Corfu. There they invented frescoes, bull-leaping and central heating, before moving on to the attractive holiday isle of Crete, famed for its olive groves, windmills and old-world Venetian ports throbbing with music, art and romantic night-life. They swiftly became mistress of the world and it wasn't long before all nations of the earth toiled beneath their tight-fisted thrall.

Nowadays, of course, Crete is part of Greece, as is well known. The colourful and friendly Cretan we see today diving for drachma or dancing the traditional souvlaki into the early hours with bus-loads of German tourists may have been born in Crete but to all intents and purposes he is a Greek with a Greek passport. Back in the misty days of the beginning of Civilization, however, the reverse was true. Seeing as Greece was *part of Crete*. In other words, the ancient Greek would have held a Cretanous passport and called himself a Cretan. In the same way that nowadays a Maltese will call himself British while a Briton would never call himself a Maltese, obviously. At least, not unless he was drunk or under torture.

I would just like to say that in certain of my previous comments I had no intention of casting any aspersions on Malta or the Maltese, which is not only another very attractive holiday resort, as is well known, but also, of course, deeply quintessential to our understanding of world history at this time.

CHAPTER XVII

THE GLORY THAT WAS MALTA

'Thou wast not born for death, immortal Isle!
No hungry generations tread thee down;
The voice I hear this passing night was heard
In ancient days by emperor and clown.'

(W. B. Keats)

RICHLY steeped in legend and antiquity, this deeply joyful, generous and fiercely patriotic people are probably the greatest nation ever known at this juncture.

They have done numerous very interesting things renowned throughout the world and are visited by many countries which is possibly why it is so crowded. Not that that matters obviously.

They also have many pulsating discotheques, safe bathing and very cheap shops, and there, sadly, we must end our all-too-brief historical tour around the glorious tapestry of Malta's past.

THINGS TO DO:

1. Make a Maltese cross.

CHAPTER XVIII
MINOS AND THE CRETANS: PART TWO

'It is an ancient Mariner,
And he stoppeth one of three.
"By thy long grey beard and glittering eye,
Now wherefore stopp'st thou me?"'

(Coleridge)

ANYWAY, as I say, Greece would have been part of Crete if Greece had existed, which it didn't, obviously, seeing as Greece came *after* Crete and not *before* it.[1] In other words, the Cretans ruled the area where Greece now is. It is, therefore, misleading to say that all Greeks were Cretans seeing as there weren't any Greeks. They would have been if there had but there weren't so they couldn't, basically. It goes without saying however that if Greece *had* come before Crete then there most likely wouldn't have *been* a Crete, seeing as Greece was much more advanced than Crete, with central heating, crockery, the Acropolis, algebra, the Olympic Games and so forth, and would have made Crete redundant before it ever got off the ground, as it were.[2]

[1] Greece at this time was, in fact, peopled by wandering tribes of bouzouki salesmen and yoghurt traders. Their origins were entirely unknown, not only to historians but also to themselves.

[2] We notice this syndrome time and again throughout history. Discoveries, inventions, whole epochs that might simply never have happened had the one that superseded it not superseded it but come before it. What if the Russian communists, for instance, had come before the Czars? Or Stone-Age man had invented the yacht before he invented the dug-out? What then? Not that he'd have needed a yacht obviously. Seeing as there was still no English Channel. At least, *hopefully* there was no English Channel, as we noted on page 26. It is, in fact, my surmise that he probably took a dug-out with him, in case he got

41

Anyway, the Cretanous Empire was very famous as we have seen, and this was mainly due to King Minos who was the Cretanous king and virtually done it all single-handed, basically. There is, however, a massive area of controversy surrounding King Minos and this concerns his age, which was very old. In fact he is recorded to have ruled Crete from 3000 to 1400 B.Ċ., which is a period of no less than sixteen hundred years! An impossible task, surely, for any one man. According to the *Guinness Book of Records*, the oldest man in the world is Shigechiyo Izumi, a Japanese pensioner and he's only 142. So how King Minos managed to live *and* rule the whole world, AND indulge in the endless appalling sexual excesses that he was supposed to have done (and which we need not go into at this juncture, thank you very much) for *sixteen hundred years* is surely a feat beyond human imagining. Nevertheless, there it is in the histories. In black and white Minoan Linear B Script:

> MINOS, King. Lord of the Seas,
> Ruler of the Earth, Master of
> the Universe. b. Ag. Nicolaos
> 3000 B.C. d. Knossos 1497 B.C.
> Education: None. Did EST
> in 1402 B.C. Failed.
> Hobbies: swimming, dancing,
> pottery, bull wrestling.

Immediately, we smell a rat. At least I smelt a rat. And for many agonizing months, during the penning of this tome, I laboured over this problem alone, venturing into the darkest recesses of the Minoan past. Delving where no historian has ever trod. Until at last I discovered what is, in my opinion, probably the most audacious cover-up the world has ever known.

For what I am now able to disclose is this:

There never was one King Minos. But many. Many King Minoses. In fact hundreds of King Minoses. All with the same name. All members of the same unscrupulous family using a single, simple and brilliant device to

---

stranded in Calais or Ostend, or somewhere with no way of getting home. On the other hand, if the English Channel *had* suddenly appeared, he could presumably have made his dug-out on the spot, as it were, rather than lug a forty-foot tree trunk halfway across Europe for a fortnight's mammoth trapping. Mind you, I can't imagine that making a family-size dug-out on a wind-swept Normandy beach with a couple of bits of old flint and a load of prehistoric babies and relatives whingeing and whining to get home, would have been a great barrel of laughs at the best of times. Not to mention his dead mammoths. So on second thoughts I should imagine he took it with him. On spec, as it were. But who will ever know? This is one of History's tantalizing mysteries that will probably always remain unsolved and all we can do is speculate.

remain in power. To convince the Cretanous electorate that the first King Minos had never died.

And he it must have been – this first King Minos – who invented this extraordinary scheme. I picture him, on his death-bed. Beneath his frescoes. His young son at his side.

'I name you . . . King Minos. You will rule the Cretans.'
'I beg your pardon?'
'I name you King Minos. You will rule the Cretans.'
'But my name is Polyeucetes.'
'No, bull's offal, you are Minos. Now I depart this life.'
'King Minos the Second?'
'No! King Minos the First.'
'Sorry?'
'King Minos the First!'
There is a pause as the beeswax candles gutter.
'But *you* are King Minos the First.'
'No, heifer's pizzle.'
'Sorry?'
'*You* are King Minos the First.'
'I am King Minos the First?'
'Yes.'
'I see.'
'Got it?'
'Yes.'
'Good. Now I depart this life.'
'So who are *you* then?'
'King Minos the First!'
'And *I* am King Minos the First?'
'Yes. But Minos the First plus a Minos is Minos the Second.'
'What?'
'And Minos the Second minus a Minos leaves Minos the First. Which is you.'

Despite the octogenarian monarch's totally collapsed lungs and proximity to death he somehow summons the strength to grasp the lapels of the boy's toga.

'Now listen, Friesian bollocks. There *is* no King Minos the First! Right?'
'But –'
'No King Minos the Second, no King Minos the Third, no King Minos the Fourth. Just King Minos. *Me!* And I will never die. *Get it?*'
'Then how will *I* be King?'
'Of course I *will* die. I'm going to die in about three minutes, aren't I?'
'Yes.'

'I'd hardly be lying here shivering under nineteen hand-woven blankets with breaths like beeswings if I was about to crack on for another eighty years would I?'

'No.'

'But *they* won't know that.'

'Who?'

'The populace, you idiot. The Cretans! As far as they're concerned, I never die.'

'So you're eternal.'

'Exactly.'

'So *I'm* eternal.'

'Right.'

'So I'm you.'

'Yes.'

'But I'm nothing like you. I'm delicate and gentle, soft-spoken and beloved of all the little creatures of field and fen. I have no time for the pleasures of the body. I am committed to a life-time of ascetic contemplation and intense self-scrutiny. I write elegiac odes on the wind-swept hillsides. I'm the complete opposite of you.'

'D'you wanna be King?'

'Well I'd rather hoped to be a kind of scholar-poet king. A kind of shepherd figure to my people.'

'D'you want to be fed to the crabs by the Opposition?'

'The crabs?'

'Lowered inch by inch into a tank full of flesh-eating crabs, solely by your knackers? Or – be a blood-soaked tyrant and the master of undreamt wealth, with a billion slaves, a different woman every night, a chariot stadium and your own private zoo?'

There is an agonized silence as the gentle tear-streaked youth undergoes a massive personality transformation.

'Okay.'

'What?'

'I'll be a blood-soaked tyrant and the master of undreamt wealth.'

'Marvellous . . . Aggh . . . now I depart –'

'But how do I explain this sudden youthing process? You are phenomenally aged with no hair and incredibly wrinkled and I am eleven.'

'Tell 'em it's magic.'

'Right.'

'Hide me under the bed and bury me at midnight.'

'Right.'

'Not now!! When I'm dead!'

'Sorry.'

'You are me now. I never was. Nor will you be. But he who comes beyond. Nor will he be, either.'

'Pardon?'

'Aggh . . .'

In this way the Minos family ruled Crete for sixteen hundred decadent and blood-soaked years. On a rough calculation and taking into account the wide variety of hazards that attended the average classical potentate, including javelin injuries, Achilles' heels, metamorphoses into animals, and odysseys, then supposing each Minos ruled for an average of fifteen years over the full sixteen hundred years, there would have been approximately 106.6 different Kings, all called King Minos. And the Cretans would have been none the wiser. This, as I say, is a pretty remarkable historical surmise and one that, to my knowledge, has not yet been presented to the historical fraternity. I expect it to rock the foundations of Minoan research and to lose me many friends.

HOW WE KNOW NO. 2

Most ancient writings were done not in words like what we have, but in little tiny pictures, known as hieroglyphics (*hiero* = little tiny, *glyphics* = pictures). Archaeologists such as myself are now able to translate hieroglyphics and so have a unique glimpse into the ancient world. Minoan Linear A Script dealt with simple words like 'cat', 'sandal', 'urn', 'Bouzouki', 'kebab', etc. Linear B Script included more advanced concepts such as, 'vague sense of unease', 'Psychoanalysis', 'Big Bang Theory', 'A pound of groceries', etc. Here is the above biography of King Minos as it was originally written:

Clearly, I am not denying the many benefits the Minoses – or Mini as they was known – brought to the ancient world. They certainly put the Aegean on the map, for example. If there had been maps. There were no maps, obviously, till aeroplanes and helicopters. But if there had been, they would have put it on it. But it would be foolish to pretend that they didn't also live probably the most depraved and corrupt life the world had yet seen, centreing around habits that, fortunately for us, have no place in a serious academic textbook such as this. Suffice it to say that I have personally seen private frescoes depicting certain adult proclivities that left me very very deeply embarrassed indeed.

Nevertheless, it wasn't all a bed of roses being a Minos.

One of them, for instance, got his come-uppance in the form of a domestic life so bitter and primally traumatic as to be almost unmentionable in this volume. And so it was that this particular King Minos had a wife called Pasiphae (so called because of her resemblance to the Pacific Ocean). And Pasiphae developed a passion for a white Hereford bull, as they quite often did in them days. Her overwhelming lust was requited and the young Hereford returned her love without hesitation. At first they would only meet in secret, shyly conversing in fields and sheds, but as their obsession grew the Queen and the Hereford began to walk quite openly through the chambers and greenhouses of the palace.

TEACHERS PLEASE NOTE:

THE REST OF THIS CHAPTER CONTAINS
MATERIAL OF AN EXPLICIT NATURE.

And then it was that they did know one another and with him it was that she did sire a son and there was great rejoicings and the King left his bull-leaping and came swiftly unto her chamber.

But then it was that it was seen by all that the young new-born infant had horns, a tail, hoofs and mooed. Thus making it reasonably obvious to anyone but an idiot that King Minos had *not* played an overly large part in this particular conception.

Immediately, the young heifer was locked in a labyrinth and fed on maidens and male models from Athens, while the King grew donkey's ears and Pasiphae went off with a Durham Shorthorn.

The Minotaur – as this little mis-shapen oddball became known – was a political embarrassment to the King, particularly seeing as he was destined to be the next Minos which was clearly a non-starter from the start.

Fortunately for the Minotaur, however, the Cretan Empire came to an end and he was discovered in a fairground by a kindly Greek doctor who took him into his home and cared for him as he own son. The Minotaur became a vegetarian and was soon the toast of Athens, mixing with actresses and orators and changing his name to Martin. Then one day he met the daughter of another illicit union. A Canada goose with the body of a maiden. They immediately fell in love and, bidding farewell to the kindly doctor, set sail for Winnipeg to raise a family of little quarter gosling calves.

THINGS TO DO:

1. Make a scale model of Crete.

2. Write an essay entitled: 'The life and training of an Athenian male model.'

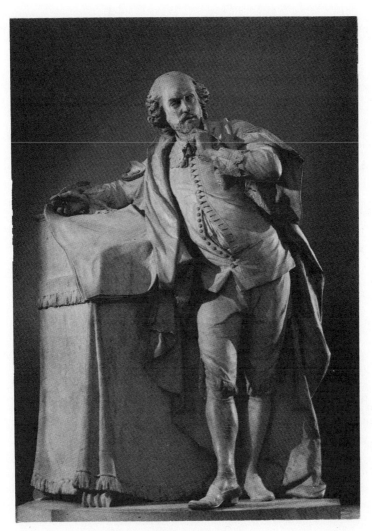

1. *William Shakespeare*
Probably the most famous man to have ever lived

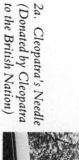

2a. *Cleopatra's Needle*
(Donated by Cleopatra
to the British Nation)

2b. *Commonwealth Institute*
(built by Cromwell to commemorate the Civil War)

2c. *Canada House*
(one of the most loved buildings in all London)

2d. *Nelson's Column (the world-famous landmark, built by the*
Arts Council to commemorate the Battle of Trafalgar Square)

2. FOUR FAMED HISTORIC VENUES

3. Miss Juliet Stevenson
Probably this country's greatest living
Shakespearian prima donna, in my opinion

4. Michelangelo's Birthplace
No. 96, Pinham Drive, Bournemouth
(see Little Known Facts No. 3)

5. Author wearing mystic Egyptian pyramid (travelling version)
(see page 157 Things to do)

6a. Toronto

6b. Leicester, upon which of course
the famed Canadian capital was modelled
(see page 109 The Renaissance)

7a. Lawrence of Arabia   *7b. Ben Hur*

7c. Lorenzo the Magnificent   *7d. Philip II of Spain*

7. FOUR HISTORICAL LEGENDS
(enacted by the author)

8a. Stage 1 (8.00 a.m.)

8b. Stage 2 (8.05 a.m.)

8c. Stage 3 (8.12 a.m.)

8d. Stage 4 (10.00 a.m.)

8e. Stage 5 (13.45 p.m.)

8f. Stage 6 (18.20 p.m.)

8. THE DESMOND DINGLE GUIDE TO BUDDHIST MEDITATION

Genuine Photographs taken during author's daily meditation (see page 114 The Life of Buddha)

WARNING: On no account to be attempted unless supervised by trained Zen Buddhist

CHAPTER XIX
CATALHÜYÜK

'He with the longest ladder has the least children.'

(Old Catalhüyükian witticism)

ONE of the first cities was Catalhüyük. This was approximately the size of Coventry and is thought to have been in Turkey, although the dots on the U's have given rise to the belief that it may well have been in Sweden.

The Catalhüyükians

The Catalhüyük people or Catalhüyükians as they was known, wore nothing but a rather crude loincloth, both in and out of the home; but this we shouldn't condemn, seeing as they was still very prehistoric in their attitudes, despite the fact that they had invented urban dwellings, rudimentary cooking utensils and an early form of lino. They lived thousands and thousands of years ago and nobody quite knows when they lived but it was certainly a long, long time anyway. So really the permissiveness in their dress and their lack of doors shouldn't be held against them. The Greeks, who lived much later, wore even less and often nothing at all and have no excuse whatsoever.

Catalhüyükian Houses

Catalhüyükian houses were one storey high with full central heating, three bedrooms and a damp course. The only drawback was there was no doors, seeing as they hadn't been invented. And for this reason they entered their houses by climbing a ladder and crawling through a special hole in the roof, which can't have been overly easy on a dark night after a couple of glasses of home-made papyrus beer, particularly seeing as all Catalhüyükian houses looked identical and nobody had invented numbers yet either. In other words, you could easily have found yourself crawling through the roof of the wrong house and falling fifteen foot onto some semi-nude prehistoric dinner party. Or worse!

Catalhüyükian House or Dwelling

The Catalhüyükians
The Catalhüyükians was, however, a very interesting people with numerous customs, one of which was to bury their dead relatives under the bed, which some of the more sensitive members of the community could have probably done without, I should imagine. They had religious reasons, obviously, which I wouldn't wish to question, but it must have been a little eerie, to say nothing of the smell in a hot climate such as Turkey. Having a meal, with all your dead grandparents going back centuries stuffed under the bed right next to where you was eating your pudding, must have been a bit unpleasant to say the least.

Catalhüyükian Houses
In our sketch we have removed part of the wall so you can see inside what a Catalhüyükian's house would have looked like (note the dead bodies). The removed wall is in order to facilitate your seeing inside, and is not a result of someone who missed the hole in the roof.

48

CATALHÜYÜK

The Catalhüyükians

The Catalhüyükians could not write, owing to the fact that they was still very ancient and hadn't heard of hieroglyphics. Neither could they read, although this is not surprising, obviously, seeing as they had nothing *to* read. For this reason there was no newspapers. However, they were an imaginative people and did invent a rather unique form of human newspaper to keep abreast of international world events, which is very important, as I should know. For this purpose a dangerous criminal was plucked out of a Catalhüyükian prison and forced to memorize all world news that was available at the time, including sporting events, the arts, women's issues, classified advertising, jumble sales and local entertainment. The criminal was then hung by his ankles in the Civic Centre while he recited the whole lot for ten or eleven hours without a break before being beaten to death by the entire audience. This happened daily, with a choice of two criminals on Sundays.

THINGS TO DO:

1. Unfortunately, not a lot happened in Catalhüyük as far as historians can glean, apart from home burials, the daily beating to death of newscasters and occasional arguments over domestic chores. (Notice also how few feature films have been inspired by Catalhüyük. *Queen Elizabeth of Catalhüyük* was planned as a Hollywood spectacular in 1940 but never got off the ground.) So it is a little hard to suggest anything for the student to do to enhance his knowledge of this fascinating period, but you might like to consider:

a) Compile a Catalhüyükian washing-up rota.

b) Write an essay entitled: 'The Contents of a Catalhüyükian lady's handbag.'

c) Paint a picture of a Catalhüyükian OAP being stuffed under the bed.

CHAPTER XX
THE GREEKS

'Θε γρεεκς ψιλλ βε ιν γρεεςε νεργ ςοον.'

(Dying words of King Minos CVI)

THE Greeks came straight after the Cretans and swept immediately into Greece, thus becoming the Greek Empire as they are to this day[1]. Hence it was they became the next major Civilization in the history of the world and are probably the most famous of all the major Civilizations we've had so far. Many historians will dispute this, I should imagine, particularly *Egyptologists* who will doubtless say that Egypt is the most famous, seeing as they invented the pyramids, Cleopatra's needle, Cairo and the Sphinx. But to this argument I would say only this: Fair enough! The Egyptians *did* invent the pyramids and so forth. Nobody disputes this.

---

[1] The reader may have noticed that the Greeks do *not* in fact come after the Cretans in this particular work. A feature pointed out by my colleague Wallace, for which I thank him. Needless to say, this is *entirely intentional* and is certainly not the result of any authorial negligence, it goes without saying. In other words, obviously I did not *forget* that I had just written the chapter on the Catalhüyükians, Wallace! I, in fact, made use here of a rather innovative literary device, employed by many famous authors such as Milton, Brontë, John Fowles and so on, who put chapters in where you *wouldn't normally have them*. It is, in fact, a very advanced form of what is known in publishing circles as *Chapter Placement* which is, of course, one of the very first things you have to learn as an author, and which is basically the art of knowing what order to put your chapters in. I think possibly it would be extremely useful for me to say the many budding authors still looking for that first lucky break like what I done, that Methuen are incredibly hot on *Chapter Placement* and it will be one of the *first* things they look for in your manuscript. In other words, if I may offer a small word of advice, *don't* just go sticking your chapters anywhere willy-nilly, as it were, just because me and John Fowles do. We've both been at this game a good few years now and we can afford to experiment. If possible, learn to get them *in the right order first*. In other words, learn to use that mighty tool with which you have been endowed before attempting to cross the Hellespont of literary controversy.

They built Abu Simbel and the pharaohs. *But are they in use today?* This is the question. How often do you see a two-thousand-foot-high pyramid in an English graveyard? How often do we use a sphinx or Abu Simbel in our common-or-garden daily life? The answer is brief but short. Never. Or at least very rarely.

The Greeks, on the other hand, invented endless essential and labour-saving things that are in use to this day. Crockery, the Olympic Games, the Coliseum, olives, words, tyranny, the Oedipus complex, hang-gliding. The list is endless. To my mind there is no question about it. Without the Egyptians we would simply be short of a couple of mummies and the Suez Canal. Whereas, without the Greeks we would almost certainly not be able to stand where we stand today, in a manner of speaking.

The Greeks are obviously most famous for what they done in Greece which they ruled (and very well, too, if I may say so) but it is my belief that they also ruled many other parts of the world as well, in particular the United States of America. This is a remarkable new theory which happens to be my own, as it happens, and I would like to take this opportunity, at this point, of pausing briefly to examine it in considerable detail at this juncture.

Did the Greeks reach America?

A quick glance at the map of the United States reveals three Corinths, thirteen Athenses, nine Spartas, five Venices and one Thermopylae. Now, I have never been one for jumping to outlandish conclusions but surely this must be more than pure coincidence. As we have already seen (*see above*), the Greeks invented nearly everything the world has ever known. So wouldn't one trip across the Atlantic have been a piece of cake to such a people?

Besides, who else but a race of deep intellectuals would have thought to call a couple of wooden shacks and an outside toilet *Athens*? Or *Thermopylae*? Which is a feat of spelling in itself. Some dice-wielding Billy the Kid, reeking of alcohol, cheroots and saddle soap? He'd have called it 'Shenandoah' or 'Moosejaw' or something equally non-classical. The point I'm making is that the very names of Athens or Thermopylae are extremely poetic, cultural and intellectual words in their own right and were clearly invented by numerous scantily-clad but very clever, bearded Greek experts who put *a great deal of time and effort into thinking them up* and not by some psychopathic gun-toting cowpoke who just happened – coincidentally – to dream it up for some derelict silver-mine in Nebraska.

Conclusion

To sum up, it is a well-known fact that the Greeks was the first people to conquer the world under Alfred the Great, the well-known king. I'm not saying he reached everywhere, obviously. But he definitely reached a lot of places.

So why not the United States of America?

War with Sparta

Unfortunately, after Alfred, Titus Andronicus, Ivan the Terrible, the Great Soprendo and all the many numerous famous Greeks who invented dictatorship, democracy, kebabs and algebra, for which they are still renowned to this day, the Greeks immediately had a very unpleasant civil war with three hundred Spartans who lived a very Spartan existence in Sparta under their leader Spartacus, the world-famous Roman gladiator and film.

Sparta, of course, was known throughout the classical world as 'The Glasgow of the South'. The three hundred Spartans themselves lived in stone council houses with no central heating or underpants and spent their lives eating Chinese take-aways, losing football matches, vandalizing civic monuments and staggering home from half-empty dance halls at three in the morning. The Spartans, however, were an immensely friendly, gentle, cultured and sophisticated people and in this way had a massive similarity to modern-day Glaswegians as it happens, who are amongst some of the finest people I have ever met in the *whole world*.[1]

The End of Greece

At the same time the Greeks all became decadent, due to excessive theatre-going and adult games which we don't need to go into at this stage, and were swiftly crushed by the Meads and Persians not surprisingly.

---

[1] Many Glaswegians have, in fact, become very famous figures, known and admired throughout history. Mary Queen of Scots, for instance, the Duke of Edinburgh, Macbeth, Scott of the Antarctic were all Glasgow-born and would be the first to admit it. While, of course, many modern-day Glaswegians are now international celebrities of world-standing. These include His Honourable the right David Steel, the world-famous Liberal; Jimmy Shand, the radio organist; Andrew Cruikshank, the celebrated doctor; and Hannah Gordon, the famous international star of stage and screen.

THE GREEKS

THINGS TO DO:

1. Build a scale model of ancient Greece.

2. Design a mural entitled: 'Life in Ancient Greece.'

3. Design an ancient Greek.

4. Write a play about the Oedipus complex in the style of Greek tragedy.

CHAPTER XXI

THE GRANDEUR THAT
WAS ROME

'Nihil est impossible, sed certain homines sunt.'

(Old Roman witticism)

THE Birth of Rome

The Romans, whom I have personally studied in great detail, were the next Civilization after the Greeks and were generally similar, wearing similar types of helmets and buildings and generally doing similar kinds of things.

Unlike the Greeks, however, the Romans were Italian.

Roman Character and Dress

The Romans were more sensible and generally older than the Greeks, most of whom – if their vases are anything to go by – wore extremely short tunics with next to no underwear that reveals more than they hid, if you get my meaning. Now the Mediterranean countries are hot, I grant you, but that's no excuse for just walking about in the nude whenever you feel like it, and is one of the major reasons why the Greeks became decadent and died out. Which is why the Romans came in of course. And a great relief to all concerned, if I may say so.

Greek Nudity

Greek nudity began, as it happens, in sporting activities which you had to do in the nude for religious reasons. This was mainly seeing as the Greek gods (Zeus, Jove, Mars, Bounty, Venus de Milo etc.) was all completely nude. As can be seen in numerous famous Greek paintings such as 'Hercules Unchained', 'Clash of the Titans', 'Venus Emerging from a Shell' by

54

Botticelli and 'Stag at Bay' by Sir Edwin Landseer. In other words, if you was a Greek athlete, you weren't even allowed so much as a pair of plimsolls. Whatever the sport, chucking the discus, pole-vaulting, lawn tennis, doing the hurdles, you had to be totally bare. Which was fine, obviously, if you had a very aesthetically beautiful body like Botticelli, or Torvill and Dean, or someone. Or me, to be honest. But a little cruel if you didn't, clearly. Like various people I know, for instance, who – without naming names obviously – have very unappealing bodies, to put it mildly.

CHAPTER XXII
THE RISE OF UR

'There are more things in Heaven and Ur,
Than are dreamt of in your philosophy,
Horatio.'

(Lady Hamilton)

ANOTHER very major Civilization which also rose at approximately this time, give or take a few years obviously, was Ur, which had momentarily slipped my mind which is hardly surprising seeing as I have quite a lot on it at the moment, actually, as would *anyone doing the whole history of the entire world*, and was identical to Catalhüyük, only without the ladders. For this reason they couldn't get into their dwellings and Ur collapsed.

THINGS TO DO:

1. Write an essay entitled: 'A trip to an Ur restaurant.'

CHAPTER XXIII
THE GRANDEUR THAT WAS ROME: PART TWO

'There's nowt as queer as fowk.'

(Cicero)

THE Decline of Greek Nudity

Anyway, most Greeks had a very attractive body, aesthetically, so it wasn't long before everyone was walking round stark naked, showing it off everywhere and putting it on vases which was, of course, the thin end of the wedge and which led, as we have seen, to the entire collapse of Greece generally, within a few days.

A Famous Greek Thinker

The only Grecian, in fact, who didn't have an aesthetically beautiful body, was Socrates, the famous Greek thinker, who, from the photos, was extremely overweight with a receding forehead and a bit of manky hair on the back of his head. For this reason, he put hemlock in his retsina and died in the bath of his Athenian hotel. He was discovered the next morning by the chamber-maid, surrounded by his dietary supplements, his exercise bicycle and his Grecian 2000.

Socrates, of course, discovered nearly everything there was to know at the time single-handed, including sculpture, triangles, disinfectant, the helicopter, ventriloquy, central heating and the fact that the bath will overflow if you get in it when it's too full. In other words, one might have thought he had enough going for him, without having to have an aesthetically beautiful body as well. I happen to know scores of people who have immensely unattractive bodies and who are also incredibly dull and boring. People, in fact, who have nothing going for them whatsoever. Like

Wallace, for instance. But they don't go round taking hemlock all over the place. They carry on with their pathetic lives as best they can. With courage and dignity and a sense of humour.

Greek Sport
The Greeks also invented athletics which they done in the Olympic Games, which they also invented.

The Olympic Games
The Olympic Games were held on the top of Mount Olympus, apart from the Winter Olympics which were held, as they are today, in Switzerland or Austria, due to the snow.[1] The Olympic Games was invented, as is well known, to unite all nations upon the Earth, but were a smaller affair than what they are now seeing as everyone else was either still very prehistoric (United Kingdom, France, Belgium etc.), didn't yet exist (Africa, Russia, India, China, Australia, South America etc.) or were only interested in board games (Crete, Egypt, Catalhüyük etc.). For this reason the Greeks constantly won all the medals, which rather defeated the object, obviously, and, as a result, became tragically spineless, which is another reason they died out, as any psychiatrist will tell you.

Reasons behind Greek sport
All Greek sports symbolised moments in Greek history. The marathon, for instance, commemorated the Battle of Marathon, while chucking the discus commemorates the Battle of Discus in which the Macedonians[2] were routed by the people of Discus, who hurled massive dinner plates at them until they ran away. The Discus dinner plate is now immortalised of course as the discus which is hurled at modern-day athletes.

The 1988 Olympics
It has just come to my attention that the next Olympics are to be held in Seoul in South Korea which, if I may say so, is probably one of the most profoundly ideal venues for the Olympic Games one could possibly hope to find. I would, in fact, just like to say to my Korean readers how deeply privileged and moved I feel at the very thought of the Olympic Games actually taking place in their historic country. It has also just crossed my mind, *en passant* as it were, that possibly the Korean Arts Council might like to consider the possibility of some kind of cultural exchange that would

---

[1] The Winter Olympics were not popular with nude Greek athletes for obvious reasons. Many ski and bobsleigh stars died horribly from exposure, and refused to compete. For this reason, the Winter Olympics waned in popularity and petered out after a few years.

[2] The Macedonians was another famous Civilization who will be sumptuously dealt with later in the volume in the Chapter entitled: 'The Splendour that was Macedonia.'

The Battle of Discus

enable two British historians, such as Wallace and myself,[1] to visit Korea free of charge, so to speak, and examine the Olympic Games from a cultural and historical point of view (with a fairly central and shaded location in the Central Stadium near the Torch if possible) while perhaps two Korean historians who aren't that interested in sport might like to examine England from, say, a more Korean point of view, with visits to our university towns and coach-trips to Stratford-on-Avon and the Lake District and Wales and so on. For this reason, it is now my enormous honour to present a brief Cultural History of Korea and the Korean peoples who, it is my opinion, are amongst the finest peoples the world has ever known, and for this reason are very similar to Glaswegians.

Wallace has just interrupted to ask if I had by any chance forgotten this chapter was on the Romans.

Once again, I should like to take this opportunity of thanking my colleague for another of his well-intentioned but I'm afraid rather unhelpful suggestions. *Of course I hadn't forgotten, obviously, Wallace.* An experienced author such as myself hardly goes round forgetting what chapter he's on, does he? Not unless he's a complete idiot. Naturally, I'm *very profoundly aware* of what I'm writing about at all times. And I see no reason on Earth why I should defend the mercurial workings of my own authorial process to anyone. Nevertheless, seeing as I'm now being mercilessly pilloried on the block for an explanation, what happened was quite simply this.

I took an authorial decision, *in all innocence*, simply to *mention* the Greeks, in as much as the information appertaining to them would – in my estimation – throw some essential light on the Romans.

Then – suddenly and without warning – something happened.

Something pretty major. Which, as any author will tell you, should, *on no account*, be prevented if it does happen. In fact, is positively dangerous to prevent if it happens, as it happens. It is called the 'Artistic Intuitive Unconscious Impulse' and obviously only very few truly major authors get

---

[1] Who are available, as it happens.

it (such as Shakespeare, Chaucer, Dante, John Fowles, Harold Pinter etc.) and is when you start writing unconsciously or in a state of hypnotic trance. Which is, in fact, how most great works of literature get written and how I wrote the last few pages, as it happens. Under the influence of a massive Artistic Intuitive Unconscious Impulse. It is, in fact, perfectly normal for famous writers, when they get an AIUI, as it is known, to change their chapters out of all recognition, and often whole books become *totally different kettles of fish* to how they started. Shakespeare, Chaucer and Dante, for instance, often had no idea what they were writing from start to finish. And no one batted an eyelid. Certainly, no one carped on and on about it *ad nauseam* for hours on end like some people I could mention.

Dante's *Divine Comedy*, for example, began as a light-hearted pot-boiler (as the title implies), then suddenly, halfway through, the Artistic Intuitive Unconscious Impulse occurred and – Wallop! – one of the most profoundly artistic plays ever written was born. Surprising everyone, not least Dante himself, who, before his mighty Quartet, was known as the Ray Cooney of the Canto.[1] In other words, what I'm saying is the truly unconscious author *cannot be held responsible* for what he writes. He just goes into a hypnotic trance and the words, of which he is totally unaware, simply surge out of his unconscious on to the paper. The result is anybody's business. The result in this case, as it happens Wallace, was in my humble opinion *some extremely useful further information about the Greeks which I personally believe many people will be very interested in*. But seeing as it has apparently caused such confusion, chaos and controversy throughout the readership, and innocent members of the public are now wandering about in the middle of the chapter helplessly lost and wondering what's going on I have decided I have no option but to begin THE ENTIRE CHAPTER AGAIN!

THINGS TO DO:

Nothing. I'm very sorry to say. Seeing as this chapter, after a considerable amount of work and research, is now rendered *entirely null and void*. I had actually thought of some extremely interesting, entertaining and stimulating things to do, as it happens, which I think many readers would have enjoyed and been profoundly enriched by. But still, they'll just all have to be put away. Back into the raging depths of the creative soup. Probably for all eternity.

[1] It now contains some of the most artistic lines ever written, many of which, e.g. 'Quindi cocito tutto s'aggelava; con sei occhi piageva, e pertre menti gocciava il pianto e sanguinosa bava', are so artistic that they have never been translated.

CHAPTER XXIV

THE GRANDEUR THAT
WAS ROME: PART THREE

*A Roman matron went to pay her taxes. She had five pounds in
one ear and a pound note in the other. What was she?
Six pounds in arrears.*

(Famous Roman Joke)[1]

ANYWAY, the Romans wore long white bath-towels, covering everything fortunately, which were called togas (from Latin *toga* = long
white bath-towel). Except for one shoulder which was bare.

Obviously not everyone wore togas, seeing as they were an insignia of
rank. Soldiers and slaves wore *tunics*, to denote their subsidiary status,
which were generally worn well above the knee, although they wore stout
underpants underneath, so as not to offend ladies as they bent over to pick
up their shopping or whilst climbing into chariots.

So why did Romans wear togas and tunics?
The reason the Romans wore togas and tunics, according to historians of
the time, was because it was very hot and trousers would have been
uncomfortable, although this argument hardly holds water if one looks at
modern-day Greece and Italy, where you don't get bank managers and
policemen and people walking about in tunics. It may be hot, but they wear
ordinary long trousers like everyone else does. Possibly trousers hadn't
been invented, although one can hardly see why it would have been so
difficult if they'd already invented viaducts and central heating. What's a
pair of trousers to a nation who build the Colossus of Rhodes and the

[1] Found in Roman cracker.

61

Sistine Chapel, if you get my meaning? Probably the main reason why Romans wore bath-towels was because they was generally obsessed by cleanliness (like modern-day Swedes), and for this reason built numerous baths wherever possible. These were called *Roman baths*. They were not like the baths in our modern-day bathrooms, however, but instead were like huge railway stations full of endless swimming pools.

Was there any famous Romans?
Yes, there were numerous very famous Romans. In fact the Romans had probably more famous Romans *per capita* than *any other Civilization we've yet had*. Julius Caesar was probably the most important famous Roman, who ruled for most of its history. After he was murdered by the Senate (an early version of the House of Commons) Rome went to the dogs, basically, and was ruled by Caligula, who was off his trolley, as his name implies, and Nero, who was grossly overweight with appalling bowels and who forced his slaves to drink the yoghurt he'd just had a bath in. If they refused, he chucked them in the leech pit. All but one chose the leech pit.[1] Another famous Roman was Hannibal who was the first man to cross the Alps on an elephant and also built Hadrian's Wall.

Julius Caesar (note toga)

[1] Bathing in dairy produce, such as milk, yoghurt and cottage cheese was often a sign of advanced decadence in ancient Civilizations. Caligula, of course, used to bathe in gravy, but this was a sign, not so much of decadence as insanity, like talking to trees and riding his horse in the bedroom, which George III also did, as it happens. Cleopatra, the fabled Egyptian queen and legend, became renowned, of course, for bathing in asses' milk. The cruel practice of ass-milking was continued in Egypt until 1953 when President Nasser had it banned in his general crackdown on vice and corruption. The same year that saw the timely end of ass-milking also saw the abolition of the gramophone, the rumba and darts. Cleopatra of course was played by Elizabeth Taylor in the famous film of the same name, during which she married Sir Richard Burton, the renowed actor and explorer.

THE GRANDEUR THAT WAS ROME: PART THREE

So how was it the birth of Rome come about?

As is well known, the birth of Rome happened in a staggeringly short space of time. One moment there was a load of decadent Greeks flopping about all over the place, going to all-night parties and so forth, then suddenly there was the Romans. Coming out of nowhere, covered in shields, hurtling about *Italia* (Italy) or *Gaul* (France) or *Hispaniola* (Scotland) in wedge-shaped formations, taking everything over everywhere, and stabbing their adversaries in the legs with their little short stabbing swords. The reason behind this meteoric rise to world power was the fact that Romulus and Remus, who found Rome, were suckled by a she-wolf. Which explains pretty cogently how she became a world power and held it in her iron-clad thrall.

However, despite the breakneck speed at which the Romans made the Holy Roman Empire, as it was known, it didn't happen overnight, so to speak. Hence the well-known phrase or saying: 'Rome wasn't built in a day.' Which is not an overly intelligent epithet, if I may say so, seeing as *obviously* Rome wasn't built in a day. No city could be built in a day. Even Milton Keynes, which is the most advanced city in the world and was built entirely by a Macintosh computer, took two and a half weeks. So clearly, Rome, which was bigger than Manchester, could never, in a month of Sundays, get built in a day!

Pompeii was destroyed in an afternoon, but that's a different story.

A delicate and sensitive dilemma

Before we allow the sunset to fall upon the dreaming spires and mystic baths of ancient Rome, I feel it would be irresponsible and cowardly not to mention and take firmly by both hands, once and for all so to speak, one of the most delicate and sensitive dilemmas in the entire history of the world. It is a question that many historians shirk from but I feel is one that has to be answered. Quite simply it is this. How was it that the Italians, whose temperament is, to say the least, *temperamental*, managed to rule and successfully dominate the entire world for so long?

I cite one brief example. Whilst on a recent cultural tour of Florentine art treasures, Wallace and myself witnessed an employee of a car rental firm on the telephone to a colleague in Palermo, with whom he was having a misunderstanding, pick up *the entire hand-set* in his bare hands and hurl it mid-conversation against the wall. Then, picking up the phone and realizing that not only the line was gone but also the phone was hanging together only by a single remaining internal wire, he dashed it once again on the black marble floor of the rental office, in front of the astonished queue of Gatwick arrivals in the airport lounge at Rimini in which Wallace and myself happened to be standing with our in-flight holdalls. I cite this as an example of behaviour commensurate with the Italian, shall we say, highly-strung personality, but hardly with the type of personality you would have *had to have had* if you was creating the Holy Roman Empire and holding the entire world in your iron-fisted glove, if you get my meaning.

AND NOT ONLY THAT!

When you think that the Romans invented wedge-shaped battle formations, endless crucial household artefacts and methodically constructed the A5 in a straight line from Chester to Marble Arch with only pick-axes and a garden roller, it does seem an extraordinary historical *volte face* (Latin = literally, a faceful of volts) that the modern-day Italian ancestor to no less than Horatio and the bridge himself still hasn't invented the three-lane motorway, the toilet seat or the rotary washing line.

Roman Slave (note tunic)

So how was it, then, that the Italians managed to rule the world? A far more likely race to have ruled the world was obviously the English, who certainly wouldn't have gone smashing phones up whenever they felt like it! Astonishingly, however, the English were actually *ruled* by the Romans! And – even more extraordinary – not only by the Romans but also by the Normans, the Saxons, the Anglo-Saxons, the Danes, the Celts, the Jutes, the Anglo-Jutes, the Picts, the Scots, the Greeks, the Egyptians, the Cretans and the Angels.[1]

In fact, how the English, who defeated Hitler single-handed with a mere handful of old aeroplanes built from park railings and balsa wood, was *ruled* by all these people, none of whom have come to anything particularly major in my opinion, is a total mystery to me and indeed to all historians throughout the world. One popular theory, which is in fact my own theory, is that perhaps England, or Britannia, as it was called, was just an unpeopled land with nobody on it and was over-run by one race after another and when that race had over-run it, and had had a look around, and

---

[1] Naturally, there *are* broken phones in England, particularly in phone boxes which are generally broken most of the time. But it is a well-known sociological fact that broken English phone boxes are simply a result of urban decay in the inner cities and have nothing to do with any *organic* national failing, I'm very happy to say.

generally conquered it, that race went home again and then another race came and did the same thing over and over again so there never was an indigenous Briton but just different races over-running England and then going home again. I personally believe, that there *were* no actual Britons until the Tudors, who was in fact Welsh and didn't arrive until 1485, when they defeated the famous hunchback king, Richard III, who murdered his father, his wife, his brother, two little princes and the Archbishop of Canterbury, and was played by Sir Laurence Olivier in the film of the same name and directed by himself as it happens and was almost certainly a milestone in cinematic history. If not the pivotal motion picture of the twentieth century.

This would explain the almost unthinkable fact that the Britons were defeated approximately once every year from the Big Bang to the Battle of Hastings and, even more unthinkably – in other words it hardly bears thinking about – that they were treated like abject slaves and generally tortured and pillaged by such monarchs as King John and the Sheriff of Nottingham.

And so we leave Rome at the height of her power with the world still held in the tight-fisted grip of her chain-mail gauntlet. Rome was also famous for the Roman Forum, Billingham Forum[1] and *Ben Hur* which is universally acknowledged as the finest motion picture ever made in the entire history of Man.

THINGS TO DO:

1. Make a Roman Candle.

HOW WE KNOW NO. 3

Did you know that the Romans left many of their crucial words which we now use to this day in our common or garden conversations? For instance, any word beginning with *pre* is certainly a Roman word. *Pre*fab, for instance, *pre*tentious, or *pre*en. Any word beginning with *bi*, such as *bi*cycle, *bi*-focal lens, *bi*le, loony *bi*n, *bi*rd, *bi*g. Any word ending in *us*, camp*us*, b*us*, thr*us*h, tr*us*s. Any word containing the words 'Rome', 'bath', 'helmet' or 'Caligula'. In fact virtually every word in the English language is Roman. Hence we do not speak English at all, but Latin.

---

[1] Also Blandford Forum.

CHAPTER XXV
THE DISCOVERY OF TIME

'But at my back I always hear
Time's winged chariot hurrying near.
And yonder all before us lie
Deserts of vast eternity.'

(Andrew Marvell)

ONE of the most important discoveries of the Romans was time. Before them there was no minutes or seconds or days or even years. In fact before the Romans, people were all over the place. They had breakfast at lunch, tea-time in the middle of the night and no concept of diaries or wall-planners. There *was* time, obviously, otherwise everything would never have begun. In other words, it was always there, but no one *knew* it was. Like electricity or leather.

THINGS TO DO:

1. Visit a well-known clock.

CHAPTER XXVI

THE MEDES AND PERSIANS

'Of al the floures in the Mede,
Thanne love I most thise floures white and rede,
Swiche as men callen daysyes in our town.'

(G. Chaucer)[1]

THE Medes and Persians were a very famous desert people who came
after the Romans and lived in the desert although they also came
before the Romans, as well, as it happens, and had numerous wars with the
celebrated Greek Alfred the Great. He often defeated them, although they
often defeated *him* and are in fact the main reason he burnt the cakes, which
he done shortly before his death in the Battle of Marathon, celebrated to this
day in the Annual London Fun Run.[2]

An incredible and little-known fact about the Medes and Persians was
that they was in fact not one but *two* entirely separate people who, after
centuries of camel-raids and well-nicking, decided to merge governments,
as in the Liberal/SDP Alliance.

The Kings of the Medes and Persians was Cyrus the Great, then Darius
the Great, then Xerxes the Great, then Catherine the Great, all of whom
looked identical apart from their hats. The great Persian Kings ruled the
earth and were worshipped as gods. This was partly because of their

---

[1] Chaucer was a successful novelist, as is well known, so how he got away with disgrace-
ful spelling such as the above is astonishing! I can safely say that he'd never have got away
with it if he'd been done by Methuens!

[2] To raise money for London hospitals. Although so many people finish up *in* hospital as a
result that it slightly defeats the object in my opinion.

Cyrus the Great   *Darius the Great*   *Xerxes the Great*   *Catherine the Great*

charismatic and magnetic personalities and partly because non-worshippers were impaled on spikes and fed to Iranian mosquitoes which are the size of lobsters. The Great King would sit on a throne moulded in the shape of a lion's head with emeralds for eyes and lapis lazuli for teeth. It was made of beaten gold and raised on the skulls of conquered warriors between two silver brassières of burning sandals.

A crucial feature of Mede and Persian society was that men and women were strictly separated, which is the main reason why the population dropped dramatically. The women lived in the harem and lounged on silk cushions in transparent lingerie while the men wandered about beating each other's brains out, as they do to this day.

IMPORTANT WARNING FOR ALL TEACHERS

THE REST OF THIS CHAPTER CONTAINS EXPLICIT SEXUAL REFERENCES AND ON NO ACCOUNT SHOULD BE VIEWED BY PUPILS BELOW THE AGE OF EIGHTEEN. THANK YOU – AUTHOR.

When it was discovered, however, that babies come through sexual proclivity and not just out of the blue on a Persian carpet so to speak, husbands and wives were allowed to meet once a year in order to do the necessary conjugations – although always under the strict supervision of three elderly lady magi who was there to keep pleasure down to a minimum and generally take notes. Even to me – a strict celibate (for religious reasons) – this would seem an unjustifiably severe moral code to have *within the nuptial home* as it were. Particularly for newly-weds. In fact, Sexual Experts have now discovered that it is a well-known fact that the frustrated sexual urge can lead to marital rows of unparalleled ferocity as well as world wars on a global level.[1]

The Second World War, for instance, would almost certainly never have occurred if Adolf Hitler had been more attractive; while the Cuban missile crisis is now seen as a direct result of Mrs Sonia Khrushchev's withholding of conjugal favours till her husband, who had just seen *The King and I*, grew his hair back. He never did and their marriage became as arid as the Gobi Desert and only the bald premier's death averted a nuclear holocaust.

And so the mighty Medes and Persians pass on down the misty corridors of History and our journey continues.

THINGS TO DO:

1. Compile a list of other global conflicts begun on account of sexual proclivity.

2. Compile a list of famous historians who, in your estimation, have a significant lack of sexual magnetism.

3. Write a powerfully erotic historical novel entitled 'The Slave Girl and the Magus' or 'A Hot Night in the Harem'.

Freud discovering a Matrimonial Disorder

---

[1] Probably the most famous Sexual Expert the world has ever known was Sigmund Freud who – via the art of hypnotism (*See illus.: 'Freud discovering a matrimonial disorder'*) – discovered that nearly all human ailments are due to a massive lack of marital conjugations or *in-home sexual conjunctivitis* as it is known technically. In his famous work *Your Dreams Foretold* by G. B. Freud, he states: 'If *in-home sexual conjunctivitis* doesn't happen which is often the case then it comes out as world wars on a global level' – almost my exact words, interestingly enough. Readers will also be fascinated to note that Freud too had a powerful sexual animal magnetism and was thus very similar to me. Naturally, if we hadn't been, we wouldn't be able to come up with our controversial and frankly erotic theories which have changed the world.

POPULAR MEDE AND PERSIAN
MISCONCEPTIONS NO. 1

Fig. 1
Baby being born to a recently married Mede and Persian couple.

CHAPTER XXVII
THE RISE OF BABYLON

*'Babylon the Great, the Mother of Harlots
and every Abomination of the Earth.'*

(The Bible)

BABYLON was the next major Civilization and was famous chiefly for being the Mother of Harlots and every Abomination of the Earth and for having Hanging Gardens. Here the rich young Babylonian nobility sipped cooled sherbets and dallied with dark-eyed slave girls who danced beneath the perfumed bowers of hibiscus and deodar, their slender naked forms just glimpsed beneath silken robes of sheerest gossamer in the hot Babylonian night, before leading the young men deep into their scented boudoirs where, divesting themselves of the last shreds of clothing and coating their soft young pubescent bodies in lustrous oils that gleamed in the bewitching firelight, they had numerous very interesting historical discussions.

Babylonian Gardening
Obviously only the nobles could afford hanging gardens.

Many of the less well-off, however, had little hanging patios which were very attractive, while the slave classes were allowed their own hanging allotments which they rented from the Council and dug at weekends when they wasn't dallying with the nobles.

Ziggurats
These were very tall buildings full of people with different tongues. For this reason no-one knew what they were and they were discontinued after a few years.

71

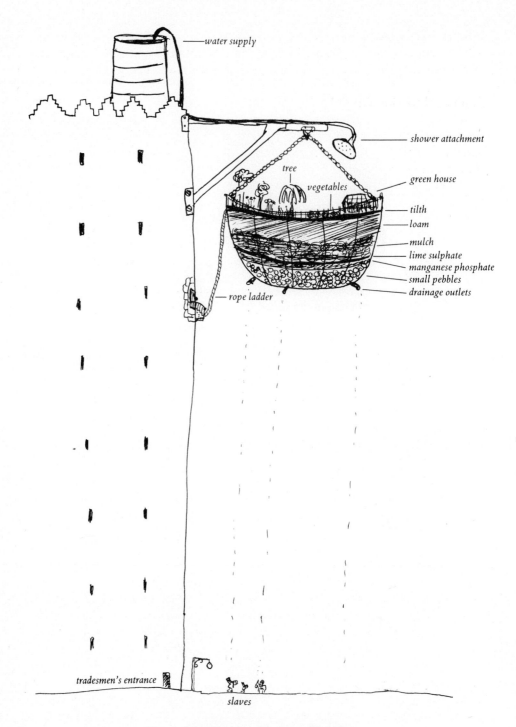

water supply

shower attachment

tree

vegetables

green house

tilth

loam

mulch

lime sulphate

manganese phosphate

small pebbles

drainage outlets

rope ladder

tradesmen's entrance

slaves

Fig. 1 *The Hanging Gardens of Babylon.*
(Note massive hanging baskets in which the gardens was hung.)

72

Other Attractions

Other attractions were Daniel's birthplace, Nebuchadnezzar's Cottage, the Fiery Furnace and Belshazzar's Feast which was held weekly.

The End of Babylon

Unfortunately, although Babylon was a horticulturist's paradise, she was also the mother of Harlots and every abomination of the Earth and for this reason was tied to a millstone and cast in the sea by a mighty angel and was found no more.

Which, Babylonogists agree, was probably a good thing all in all.

THINGS TO DO:

1. Construct your own Hanging Garden (see easy-to-follow instructions opposite). Amaze your neighbours. Make them GREEN with envy!

2. Build a Mede.

CHAPTER XXVIII

THE SCYTHIANS AND MONGOLS

'Refuse to be discouraged,
Refuse to be distressed,
For when we are despondent
Our life cannot be blessed.'

(Helen Steiner Rice – *Just For You*)

THEN, suddenly, there rose up the most dreaded nation the world had yet seen at that juncture. This was the Scythians and Mongols who lived on the vast treeless plains of Mongolia and Scythia.

The dreaded Scythians and Mongols were a race of fierce horsemen who were nomads. In other words, instead of building cities and central heating and pyramids and so forth, they spent their day pounding about on horses, playing polo, catching more horses, strapping their enemies to the hooves of other horses and basically pitching their tents wherever they felt like it.

Intriguingly, the dreaded Scythian dwelling-place was not called a 'tent' but a *Yurt* and was made of numerous skins nailed to a wooden frame. Although where they got the wood for the frames from is a total mystery, seeing as the plains where they lived were of course treeless (*see above*). They probably nipped across to the Black Forest and got them there. With some gateaux I shouldn't wonder!

Seriously, the yurt was in fact the centre of the Scythian and Mongol's life and the richer he was the bigger his yurt. Genghis Khan, for instance, had a yurt the size of Bradford.

Despite their legendary tortures and unkempt appearance, the Scythians and Mongols were obsessed with hygiene and their yurts were spotless. There was in fact nothing they liked better than putting up a clean yurt. While younger members of the tribe were always horribly punished for having a dirty yurt. For special occasions, like Coronations and Christmas and so forth, they lived in dress yurts but when they was just touring round they lived in casual yurts.

The Scythians and Mongols are chiefly remembered for the fact that they invented trousers, presumably so as not to chap the inside of your legs, seeing as they were on horses all day.

The Scythians were basically similar to the Mongols with similar hobbies, customs and yurts. The chief difference being that the Mongols were bald. There were many famous Scythians and Mongols, like Ghengis Khan to name but a few. There was also Kublai Khan, his grandson, and Tamburlaine, who wasn't a relative.

Tamburlaine

Tamburlaine was originally called Timothy, which is one of the main reasons why he didn't get anywhere as a tyrant for many years. Fortunately for him, however, he suffered an Achilles' tendon while playing polo, which meant he got called 'Timothy the Lame' or 'Tim the Lame' by the other Scythians and Mongols. And it was only a matter of weeks before the rather slurred and unattractive Scythian and Mongol dialect changed his name to 'Tamburlaine' which is a whole different kettle of fish to Timothy, obviously, if you want to rule the world.

Also, and more profound in its historical significance, the fact that he had an achilles tendon meant that he was in a foul mood all day so he went around the world punishing and pillaging more nations than he would have if he hadn't had the tendon. It is interesting at this juncture to note how many tyrants have or had physical abnormalities. Richard III, for instance, with his world-famous hunch; Napoleon with his missing hand; all of the Third Reich with their numerous reproductive difficulties; and Oedipus Rex, of course, the famous Greek King who had a famous bad foot which he got after he was manacled to a hill for thirty years by his parents.

Oedipus Rex

Oedipus, of course, wasn't so much famous as a tyrant. In other words he didn't try and rule the world or something, but is instead celebrated for founding the world-famous neurosis that many people suffer from to this day, namely killing your father and marrying your mother – which is still a fairly tyrannical thing to do, obviously, particularly if the parents in question are not willing.

Which Oedipus' parents weren't.

At least his father wasn't.

Hence the world saw the birth of psychiatry.

The Birth of Psychiatry

As is well known, Oedipus didn't know his father was his father. Or his mother for that matter. And that – in a nutshell – is *the whole point* of psychiatry, as any psychiatrist will tell you. I have studied under some of the leading psychiatrists of our time[1] and my researches have made this pretty clear to me: the basic point of psychiatry is that we do things *unconsciously*. In other words, we do things *without realising we're doing them.* And when we start doing this, we go to a psychiatrist. And as soon as possible. Not in *every* case, obviously. For instance, when we unconsciously leave a Russian novel on a bus, which I have done periodically in my life. But if we suddenly went unconsciously berserk in the High Street and slew numerous people with a chain-saw, then obviously we'd be pointed to the nearest analyst's couch, not to mention the nearest Broadmoor, which, in my opinion, many so-called neurotics might as well go to in the first place and be done with it.

The Heritage of the Scythians and Mongols

Thus it was that the Heritage of the dreaded Scythians and Mongols is trousers, polo and psychiatry.

THINGS TO DO:

1. Make a scale-model of a treeless plain.

2. Write an essay entitled 'How I would go unconsciously berserk.'

3. Who do you know who you think should see a psychiatrist?

4. Do you think *you* should see a psychiatrist?

5. Go and see a psychiatrist.

---

[1] I would just like to reassure readers at this juncture that while I have *studied* psychiatry in considerable depth for the purposes of this volume (and even become, in my own humble way, rather an accomplished psychotherapist if I may say so), I have never had to *see* a psychiatrist, obviously, I'm very happy to say. And would just like to make absolutely clear that I have never in my life had any psychiatric disorders. In fact I have had assurances from numerous leading psychiatrists that I am one of the most balanced people they've ever met. Not that there's anything *wrong* in seeing a psychiatrist. All I'm saying is I don't need one and I think it's only fair to make this clear to my readers so that they know they're in safe hands. How would it have been, for instance, if, halfway through *The History of the English-Speaking People*, Winston Churchill had suddenly announced he was a raving psychopath! Well, I, for one, would have sent it *straight* back to my lending library!

CHAPTER XXIX
THE DARK AGES

'For sheer darkness, the Dark Ages left all other ages standing.'

(Botticelli)

AS soon as the Holy Roman Empire collapsed, with all the buildings falling down and bricks and columns everywhere and everyone lying about dead in the street from drink or plague and pestilence with their teeth dropping out, a new kind of people, more terrifying than any previous kind of people, swept through a Europe still rank with the aroma of death. This people were the dreaded Barbarians, also known as the Goths and Vandals who, as the name implies, was not exactly interested in macramé or ornamental egg-colouring.

They was, in fact, to all intents and purposes, virtually identical to the Scythians and Mongols mentioned in the last chapter with yurts, carnivorous horses, bald heads and ear-rings. However, as my colleague has just this moment pointed out – for which I should once again like to thank him – they were also very different, obviously. Seeing as the Mongols come from Mongolia and the Goths come from Goth, and anyway the Mongols and Scythians lived a thousand years previous to the Goths and the Vandals and was an indigenous oriental race whereas the Goths and the Vandals was more a conglomerate of Northern tribes. I didn't say they was identical anyway, Wallace. I said they was VIRTUALLY identical. Obviously, if I had ALL THE TIME IN THE WORLD, I could describe in detail every minute difference between the two races. But it is a little difficult when not only are you writing a *Complete History of the Entire Human Race*, which is not exactly *Noggin the Nog* if you get my meaning, but you've also got some simpering secretary phoning up every ten minutes saying Sir Geoffrey Methuen doesn't understand the chapter on the Cretans and why have you left the Aryans out (whatever that is) and is there enough detail in 'The Romans'? Enough *detail*? It's PACKED with detail!

I have no wish to be disrespectful to Sir Geoffrey who, I know, is in his nineties and is not a well man, but *he* hasn't had to spend weeks and weeks of his life sacrificing hours of sleep and nearly all his leisure pursuits researching such things as the *Romans*. As it happens! Does he think I enjoy it!? Hacking through the history of the world day in day out till I'm blue in the face? Alone in my attic? Catching tuberculosis from lack of food?

Anyway, you couldn't get any more detail than I've got about the Romans. There isn't anything else *known* about the Romans. Maybe a purist might spot a couple of mini-omissions but, short of personally interviewing every Roman that ever lived, you couldn't ask for a more detailed examination of Roman history and Roman society and Roman life generally.

Also, I would just like to say that it was my own decision to leave out the Aryans, seeing as, in my estimation, although being very interesting, it has no essential relevance to this work.

Obviously, as I say, I'm not knocking Sir Geoffrey Methuen, who is one of the greatest men who ever lived, if I may say so, and is responsible for bringing the printed page and many mighty, celebrated authors such as D. H. Lawrence, Milton and myself before a wider public. But an artist is not helped by being criticized mid-*oeuvre*, as it were, when he's still in an extremely sensitive and delicate frame of mind.

Besides which – I wasn't going to mention this but I now feel I have no option – Wallace promised *faithfully* to unblock the sink. This was so as to remove the awful smell from the kitchen which has been there for the last three days. But as far as I can see he hasn't even *taken the plunger out of the Utility Room*.

If he wanted me to do it all he had to do was ask. Even though I do let him rent his room at a colossally reduced rate on condition he does all the household chores!

Anyway, he distinctly *told* me he'd do it and now, as far as I can see, he's fed all his rabbits and just gone out without so much as a by-your-leave. So not only am I writing *The Complete History of the Entire World* alone and unaided but I am also facing a constant firing squad from the publisher AND HAVING TO UNBLOCK THE KITCHEN SINK, seeing as the smell of whatever's in there is so bad that we can barely use the toilet which happens to be *through* the kitchen, as it happens. At least mine is through the kitchen. Wallace's, of course, is in the garden. So he doesn't *have* to smell it.

What I'm saying is that, owing to unforeseen circumstances entirely beyond my control, I do not unfortunately have the time to go into the minuscule differences between the Scythians and the Mongols and the Goths and the Vandals – who died out *anyway* after a few years – not unless I have a cardiac arrest due to stress which will mean that this will be a rather *short* history of the entire world.

Anyway, the Goths and the Vandals basically didn't give a toss about *anything*. They just came in and raced through Europe anywhere they fancied, desecrating graves, nicking art works, robbing pyramids and despoiling Roman baths. Which were, of course, despoiled anyway owing to all the unpleasant things the Romans done in them during the Decline and Fall of the Roman Empire.[1]

Fortunately, in the Renaissance, they were all disinfected and cleaned by the popes and Borgias and so forth, as they are to this day. As in Bath, for instance, in Wiltshire, which is now a very pleasant historical landmark, where you can gently stroll round at your leisure recalling moments from its classical heritage and having tea in the Pump Room – which Wallace and I have done on numerous occasions, as part of our researches.

HOW WE KNOW NO. 4

The Goths, fortunately, didn't last long, seeing as they were always on the move. Now nothing remains of this barbaric folk apart from their memory and their name, now absorbed into modern place names such as Gotham Moor, Gotherington, Gothers, Gouthwaite, Goyt's Moss, Gozzard's Ford, Gospel Oak, Goodwood, Grantham, Grimsby and Hull. Probably the most famous Goth and Vandal, of course, was Attila the Hun, who spent his entire day riding round all the old bits of the Roman Empire drinking and laughing and spitting and arm-wrestling and submitting anyone he found to appalling indignities beyond imagining. Goth, Visigoth, Roman or Gaul, he didn't give a tinker's elbow who they were, as long as he gained pleasure from committing horrible atrocities on them. To cut a long and disgusting story short, Attila the Hun was no Bernadette of Lourdes.[2]

Attila the Hun

[1] Recognized by historians the world over as one of the nastiest and most unpleasant periods the world has ever known. And featured of course in the world-famous novel of the same name by Stanley Gibbons. The closest modern parallel to the Decline and Fall of the Roman Empire would be a compulsory New Year's Eve Party in Trafalgar Square, full of two hundred and fifty thousand Scottish football supporters, all incredibly drunk and being sick everywhere, going on without pause for three hundred years, with the rest of the West End permanently collapsing behind it and all the public toilets closed. The Decline and Fall of the Roman Empire was also filmed, of course, with a glittering bevy of international celebrities including Omar Sharif, as it happens.

[2] St Bernadette, the famous singing nun of Lourdes, was, of course, originally Bernadette Peters of Lourdes, a famous French peasant girl who saw St Mary in a cave as she cycled

Finally, after destroying all remains of the glorious Civilization that had gone before, apart from Stonehenge, the Mona Lisa, St Paul's Cathedral and Cleopatra's needle, Attila died of a heart attack, having just won the world arm-wrestling championship at the Istanbul Olympics in A.D. 504 Attila was, in fact, ninety-two years of age, totally blind, permanently bed-ridden and under heavy sedation, but he always won the world arm-wrestling championship, seeing as whoever beat him was nailed alive on a yurt frame.

Thus it was that the Dark Ages covered the Earth, about which nothing are known, obviously, seeing as the Barbarians couldn't write and anyway would probably only have scrawled obscenities on temple walls and bus shelters, if they could have. The truth is that probably very little happened in the Dark Ages. With Attila the Hun and so forth riding about breaking everything, the best thing was probably to keep quiet, which is what most people did. They lived in little daub and wattle huts, had babies, grew maize, had a cow, talked about this and that, went swimming, visited neighbours and died. And that was life in the Dark Ages. Apart from the celebrated Byzantine Empire in the East which was famous for its icons and emperors with rectangular heads.

Monks

The only people, in fact, who was up to anything at all was the monks, who risked life and limb illuminating gospels in the Outer Hebrides. Although these took centuries to do because everything was so dark and most of them was half blind anyway, seeing as they worked too close to the page.

One of the most famous gospels was *The Book of Kells*, which had seven hundred monks working on it. They worked on it for six hundred years and had only reached the Flight into Egypt when they all got massacred by the Vikings, who are the next major people after the Dark Ages, as we shall see.

---

home from work and has been there in a frozen trance ever since. Seeing as to see a saint is a miracle, she was immediately *made* a saint, as is anyone French who happens to see a saint. The reason that seeing a saint is a miracle is that a) you can't be a saint unless you're dead so b) if you see a saint, you're seeing someone who's dead; so it's a miracle and therefore you become a saint yourself. Although only after *you* are dead, obviously. In other words, Bernadette being made a saint *immediately* is an exception, although she doesn't actually know she's a saint, of course, seeing as she's still comatose. Now she is the French patron saint of health and each year millions of people cross the globe to visit her as she stands motionless beside her bicycle. All saints are a patron saint of something and you pray to them for specific things: St Francis for animals, St Christopher for travelling, St Bernard for winter sports, St Pancras for railways, St Michael for underwear, St Aloysius for cauliflowers and St Valentine for obvious reasons.

THE DARK AGES

The Vikings sold *The Book of Kells*, which was useless to them seeing as you couldn't eat it, to the British Museum for a Friesian bull, six bags of maize and a Fabergé Egg, where it is to this day and can be viewed. It is very beautiful, obviously, seeing as that's all the monks did all day, although the last pages are in a terrible state, seeing as they was all blind by this time and fumbling about all over each other's pages.

And so the Dark Ages came to an end. And about time too, in my opinion.

THINGS TO DO:

1. Make a Dark Age daub and wattle hut (*see* easy-to-follow instructions below):
   a. Make daub
   b. Mix wattle
   c. Erect little daub and wattle hut
   d. Put in little tables and chairs
   e. Connect little phone
   f. Put in little pictures and ornaments.

CHAPTER XXX
THE VIKINGS – SCOURGE OF EUROPE

*'It often shows a fine command of
language to say nothing.'*

(Celestial Seasonings Herb Teas)

THE Vikings are celebrated for their massacres and various pillaging which they done not only to monks but also to everyone else, as is well known. This was mainly due to the fact that they lived in Scandinavia. Seeing as Scandinavia is appallingly cold with about one and a half weeks of daylight a year and the Vikings were cooped up for months on end in their huts, full of goats, hens, babies and OAP Vikings, and thus became incredibly aggressive for obvious reasons.

Viking huts were earthen mounds covered in bits of old goat skin and had turf on the roof which they put their cows on. This, however, was a thoughtless and often dangerous practice, seeing as the cows were periodically falling *through* the roof and thus through the ceiling, which played havoc with the milk yield, obviously, seeing as the Viking cow lived in a state of more or less permanent anxiety with regard to the stability of his grazing.

The Vikings, therefore, had very little milk. Not only because of the collapsing roof syndrome but also because of the Viking grass which is known, of course, to this day, as *tundra* (Old Norse: *tun* = grossly inedible grass; *dra* = like old lino). The closest relative to tundra in this country being the astro turf which they put under the fruit displays in greengrocers. So it is hardly surprising that the Vikings went off and pillaged everywhere, with all the pent-up rage that was penting up and up during the dreadful Arctic winters and all the goats and OAPs and collapsing roofs and babies and nothing to do all day except throw Rune stones which were like the I Ching, only worse.

The I Ching

The I Ching is the famous book of Chinese prophecy, which I have personally studied, by which you can see into the future. As I say, I have personally made a great study of this work, which I find somewhat over-rated, due to the fact that it tends to be somewhat unspecific in its replies. For instance, you may ask: 'Should I give the outside of the house a new coat of Sandtex this year or should I leave it until next year?' The answer to this question will probably be something like:

> 'He who rides the chariot with one wheel goes to visit the high
> priest and takes him gifts of mango and lychee; the priest smiles
> and puts them in his pocket and falls down a deep well. The
> storm that covers the goose drowns the rabbit.'

Now fair enough. I can interpret this, after three or four hours of close scrutiny, seeing as I have the training and was in fact once a Chinese monk in the Fifth Dynasty, but to the average common-or-garden man-in-the-street, who just wants to know whether to slap a coat of Sandtex up or not, it leaves a lot to be desired.

The I Ching can also be extremely depressing. 'Should I have a boiled egg or muesli this morning?' could well receive the reply:

> 'The river breaks its banks and kills all the inhabitants.'

which could put you off breakfast for good.

Mind you, as I say, compared with the Viking Runes, the I Ching is a day out at Butlins.[1] The Rune Stones are, in fact, probably the most depressing clairvoyant aid the world has ever known. They come in a small maroon bag with an accompanying booklet and here are some of the so-called ancient insights they have to offer:

> 'You are stuck in a deep rut.'

> 'You seek only your own glory.
> And lust after the world's riches.
> You put yourself alway before the needs of another.'

> 'You have covered your head with a heavy veil.'

> 'A spiritual winter is upon you.'

Which are very stupid, not to say irresponsible things to say to someone who might well be in an impressionable state. Particularly someone they've never even met! I have, in fact written to the publisher of this particular item

[1] The world-famous Holiday Camp.

(NOT Methuen's I'm very happy to say. Methuen's would never get themselves mixed up in *this* kind of mumbo-jumbo), suggesting that they take them immediately off the bookstalls as they could easily get into the hands of youngsters or people with depressions who might start taking them seriously. Obviously, I didn't draw these particular runes from the bag, *personally*. I just happened to notice them, *en passant* as it were, during my researches. Anyway, I wouldn't have believed them even if I had drawn them.

Modern Scandinavia

Nowadays, of course, the Scandinavians have pine furniture and saunas. Every fourth person you meet is an architect, and disease has been eliminated. However, despite these benefits they are generally an unhappy and depressed people due to the genetic memories of eleven and a half months of OAPs, runes and tundra still coursing like an endless death march through their veins.

The word 'joke' is unknown in Scandinavian. As are 'laughter', 'pier', 'Variety Show', and 'ventriloquist'. The only entertainers in Scandinavian showbiz history, apart from August Strindberg and the Brontë sisters, was Nina and Frederick, the famous singing duo. While a look at other famous Swedes and Danes will show you how consistently depressed they are. Ingrid Bergman the famous film director makes films about death, plagues and crumbling marriages, while Henry Ibsen and Henry Chekhov, the famous Norwegian play-writing team, wrote obsessively about suicidal ornithologists and forest clearance. As is well known, the Scandinavians are a deeply hygienic race and visitors to Denmark will immediately recall the famous Copenhagen Launderette Riots that brought the city to its knees in 1951. Their toilets smell like pine forests which is very laudable, obviously, although I have to admit that I find their use of recycled toilet paper a little hard to handle.

Danelaw

The Vikings finally left Scandinavia and moved to England where they invented numerous settlements such as London and established their own legal system called Danelaw, which was basically that anyone who didn't give a Viking what he wanted got killed.

Viking Burials

Vikings were buried at sea in a burning ship or *skip*, which, of course, is Old Norse for 'boat' (and nothing to do with the modern-day *skip* that builders chuck their rubbish in and are usually parked directly outside your house or being unloaded for hours on end blocking the only exit out of a cul-de-sac when you're incredibly late for a meeting).

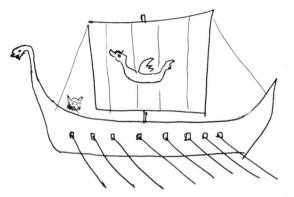

Viking ship or skip

Modern-day skip

The End of the Vikings
Numerous Viking words still remain in the English language: they include 'victim', 'viscount', 'vicar' and 'Vicenza' – the famous Italian town.

THINGS TO DO:

1. Draw up a petition against the use of skips in residential streets. For free ANTI-SKIPS newsletter send to:

   Managing Director
   Methuen Books Ltd.
   New Fetter Lane
   London E.C.1.

2. Write a four-act play about a deeply depressing Scandinavian love affair on a fjord.

CHAPTER XXXI
THE BIRTH OF ENGLAND

'If I should die, think only this of me:
That there's some corner of a foreign field
That is for ever England.'

(Peter Brook)

ENGLAND is universally acclaimed as one of the greatest countries the world has ever known. This is chiefly due to the undeniable fact that never once throughout our proud history have we been invaded since 1066, which is over nine hundred years. Although there is a new contemporary theory gaining in credence with leading historians, which is my own theory as it happens (outlined in detail in Chapter XXIX), that we *couldn't* have been defeated in 1066 seeing as we didn't actually arrive until 1485.

But even if we *was* here and *did* happen to get invaded by the Normans who, if I may say so, already had a few years behind them inventing the crossbow and the siege engine and so forth (while we was busy dredging the fens and making the place a little bit habitable to live in, as it happens!) – *so what*!? Who happens to care? Because I certainly don't! And certainly won't be losing any sleep over it, thank you very much. Nine hundred invasion-free years is a boast few other countries can make, since they have all been invaded probably more times than they care to remember.

Foreign historians obviously try and put this unique and remarkable fact down to the fact that we are an island surrounded entirely by water, but are wilfully choosing to forget the *two* ingredients essential to our national success story which is (a) our extraordinary tenacity in adversity which has kept the invader from our doors for so long and will continue to do so for ever more, may I say, and (b) our remarkable powers of invention like the printing press, tarmac, electricity, gravity, astronomy and North Sea Oil to name but a few.

The gifts of sheer inventiveness that we have showered on the world are too numerous to mention in this volume and the great and noble men and women sired on our shores likewise. Shakespeare, Nelson, Queen Victoria, Beethoven. The list is endless. Great British men and women who have sacrificed all, often their lives, to make this world a better and richer place in which to live.

It would not be unfair to say that nearly everything and everyone of international importance was discovered or born in England.

A Moving English Story

Once upon a time the famous historian and monk, the Honorable Bead[1] was standing in the busy market-place of some early British town. We are not told the name of this town but it is my belief that the town was *our own capital* London and the market-place in which he stood was none other than probably the most famous market-place in the world, Covent Garden, the celebrated fruit and veg market with its fashionable boutiques and restaurants, not to mention the London Transport Museum with its legendary collection of buses and tubes. It is unlikely to have been any other city, seeing as – apart from London – all other urban centres of the time was just a cluster of wattle huts on stilts in the middle of a lake, so wouldn't have had the fiscal wherewithal to build a market-place or pedestrianised precinct in the first place. Due to the massive amount of timber and stilts required to build it, not to mention the colossal roof in case of rain, which it did a great deal in those days, seeing as we was only just out of the Ice Age and is why there were so many lakes in the first place. And so it was that Bead paused awhile in this famed spot. Possibly to have his lunch at one of the many attractive pavement cafeterias. Or watch a medieval mime artist, perhaps, or a troupe of alternative jugglers. Or simply to hold forth to an audience of enraptured monks about the discovery of all human knowledge which he, of course, had recently fathered and for which he is *revered to this day*.[2]

And as he held forth there in London's own Covent Garden, which in the eyes of many famous poets and historians is the centre of the entire world, Bead made possibly his most poignant discovery. THE INVENTION OF THE VERY NAME OF ENGLAND.

And how fortunate we are that our name was discovered by one such as he and not a lesser man. We could have had *any* name. We could have been called *Siberia*, for instance. Or *Belgium*.

[1] Or Bead the Obscure, as he was known.

[2] Wallace has asked me to point out the possibility of the covered precinct in Birmingham's Bullring as the scene of this legendary moment honoured throughout the world. But – as I have pointed out to him – although Birmingham has always been a major part of our cultural heritage, the Bullring, with all due respect, is a modern affair, obviously, and didn't come in till after the Armada, as the name implies. And for this reason, therefore, must be ruled out as a possible venue for this historic moment.

Or *Honolulu*! Could we seriously have faced the Armada if we had been called Honolulu?

'What are those ships on the horizon, Admiral Barcelona?'
'Just the Honolulu fleet, your Majesty.'
'The what?'
'The Honolulu fleet.'
'Ha ha ha ha!'

OR:

'Excuse me Emperor Bonaparte?'
'Yes, General?'
'We've just heard that the Honolulus have reached Waterloo.'
'The who?'
'The Honolulus.'
'Ha ha ha ha!'

Could we seriously, in other words, have conquered half the known world, built St Paul's Cathedral, invented the Davy lamp and defeated the Japanese Empire single-handed in grass skirts, playing Hawaiian guitars and handing out garlands of flowers to all and sundry? Besides which, of course, someone else was called Honolulu. So half our history would have been taken up with endless time-wasting and costly legal battles to establish who thought of it first, while *everyone else* was inventing electricity, fighting Napoleon and running the Industrial Revolution and so forth.

Anyway, suddenly Bead espied a group of flaxen-haired youths idling about the Piazza. Watching a busker. Chucking matches down his saxophone.

'But who are these youths?' asked the mystic, struck by their fair appearance.

'Just ordinary common-or-garden, run-of-the-mill Britons,' replied the monk.

'But I am a Briton and *I* am not like these.'

'That is because you are a very *ancient* Briton, your holiness.'

'So am I not as beauteous as they?'

There was an agonised silence. Seeing as Bead had a huge nose, tiny ears, one eye four inches lower than the other and teeth like a rusty comb.

'I beg your pardon?'

'Am I not as beauteous as they?' His voice as tiny as a child.

'Of course, your Highness.'

'I am?'

'Definitely.'

At this the asthmatic seer rose. He swept over to the boys in his purple robes and gaiters and offered them his ringed hand.

'Angels!' he exclaimed. 'Thou art nothing short of angels!'

Their reply has not survived. Neither would Bead probably if he hadn't had his monks with him. The youths were not to be seen for dust while, unperturbed, the lop-eyed prelate stood in the precinct (probably outside Tuttons) in the midst of his monks, and made the historic pronouncement: 'From henceforth our nation will be called Angels because that is what we truly are, even me, am I not?'

There was another terrible silence that you could have cut with a meat cleaver. Then the song of a Dickensian lavender seller broke the terrible tension and Covent Garden resumed as if nothing had happened. Most people standing by probably wouldn't have understood, anyway, seeing as they'd have been tourists, but in that moment England was born.

For the monk wrote not 'angels' but 'angles', mis-spelling it, as they did in those days, seeing as they only had a very rudimentary education and there was no schools, obviously. Just various tonsured mystics wandering the countryside, teaching their own self-taught learning beneath leafy English bowers to rows of eager acolytes who didn't give a toss about the spelling as long as they got the facts down.

Anyway – nearly all of Shakespeare's spelling was wrong. Now this may sound absurd to those who revere Shakespeare as the greatest writer ever to put pen to paper (or quill to parchment, to be precise!)[1] Which he is, of course. In fact in my opinion he is probably the greatest person to have ever lived.

However, I have to say that I was recently shown by an academic colleague a highly secret version of Shakespeare's plays known, for some reason, as the First Folio edition and spelt exactly as Shakespeare wrote it. Obviously I am not at liberty to say where he got his hands on this document, but I can say that it left me very deeply shocked indeed.

For it is written as though by an illiterate four-year-old child. With nearly every word spelt wrong. Not to mention the grammar and punctuation which is all over the place. Obviously modern schoolchildren are not shown this otherwise, with such an example, all hell could break loose in English classrooms throughout the country, let alone the world. Anyway, for this reason, Shakespeare – and in the nick of time, if I may say so – has been cleaned up and spelt correctly, so to speak, so the general public is, of course, none the wiser.

Miss Juliet Stevenson

I have recently had the deep personal honour of interviewing Miss Juliet Stevenson, who, in my opinion, is one of the finest actresses in the land, and

---

[1] Obviously not all writers have used pen and ink. The Vikings used whalebone and blubber to write their sagas while the famous Greek dramatists used stone and chisel which is why they only wrote one play every four years. This also explains why their plays are so long, seeing as, once written, they were rarely prepared to do re-writes.

is a *prima donna* of the Royal Shakespeare Theatre at Stratford-upon-Avon, tragically burnt down in the Great Fire of London and rebuilt by Sir Peter Hall before doing the National Theatre, of course, and many operas and so forth for which he is famed throughout the theatrical world.

One of the many very pertinent topics we touched upon in her most attractive dressing-room suite was the question of Shakespeare's spelling and grammar and she personally told me that she is highly relieved that he *is* being spelt correctly, even though that's not how he wrote it, otherwise the great actors and actresses of this country, of which she is clearly one and will go a long way, if I may say so, wouldn't understand the half of what he's saying and therefore couldn't make head nor tail of it and would never learn the lines; and Miss Stevenson has had a few to learn in her time, I can tell you, besides playing a wide bevy of Shakespearian parts including Juliet, Isobel, Shylock and Heathcliff.

Whilst studying Shakespeare, I have also recently been considerably surprised at the fact that quite a lot of him doesn't make much sense either, particularly to the modern reader. I have therefore taken it upon myself to 'translate' some of Shakespeare's plays for the contemporary audience into a more popular idiom, which I hope will also assist the Bard in perhaps clearing up certain difficult bits that maybe in those days he didn't have the grammar or the education to make as clear as what I have done now today.

Here is an example of one of his famous speeches rendered into modern English, done by myself:

'To be or not to be alive.
That is the question that I am asking at this juncture.
What I'm wondering is
Whether what I should be doing is basically suffer all
the problems in my life and put up with them, as it were,
or not to.
To die or sleep is what's on my mind.
I could say, obviously, if I did this, I would have no more
concerns, no more personal problems or financial worries
but on the other hand, I would be dead.'

This is an extract from my own version of one of Shakespeare's best-known, although I tend to think rather over-rated, works, *Hamlet*. The plot tends to get a little bit convoluted and tangled towards the end and leaves most people wondering what on earth's going on. However, I am also in the process of completing a modern-day interpretation of *The Merchant of Venice* re-titled *Portia's Portions*; a musical science fiction version of *Twelfth Night* entitled *Death Star*; and a comic version of *King Lear* for popular audiences, entitled *Keep Your Hair On Lear*. All with a view to hopeful staging by one of the major companies.

The End of the Birth of England

And so it was that Bead saw a number of youths, called them 'angels', which got mis-spelt as 'angles' and so we was called England. A very beautiful tale from the beginnings of our Island Story.

THINGS TO DO:

1. Make a wall-chart entitled: 'The Greatness of Bead.'

2. Make a scale model of Birmingham as it would have looked on stilts.

3. Write this chapter in your own words.

WARNINGS:

DON'T go off to your local lending library asking for the First Folio of Shakespeare, because you won't find it. There is only one original, obviously, and that is in St Mary Magdalen College in Cambridge, safely under lock and key. Some libraries do have copies, but these can only be viewed by *bona fide* experts with written permission from the police.

DON'T go writing to famous actresses like Miss Stevenson asking for interviews and so forth. She granted one to me seeing as I am a famous author, but most of her day is spent learning lines and going to mime classes and so forth. So she has precious little time to answer reams of puerile questions all day long.

CHAPTER XXXII

THE FOURTEENTH CENTURY

'Lives of great men all remind us
We can make our lives sublime,
and, departing, leave behind us,
Footprints in the sands of time.'

(Henry Wadsworth Longfellow)

AFTER the Vikings was the Battle of Hastings and then came the fourteenth century, which is one of the most famous centuries in the world. It is chiefly famous, of course, for the Black Death, in which you started off with diarrhoea and ended up dead, covered in boils, and Courtly Love, in which you sent flowers and wrote ballads and got killed and so forth for a Lady but couldn't *do* anything, if you get my meaning.

You could to your wife, obviously, but she wasn't your Lady. Your wife was just ordinary, who you did the hoovering with and so forth. Your Lady, on the other hand, was staggeringly attractive, unblemished as snow and you would crawl through nettles stark naked, or anything else she requested, just so as you could hold her hanky. Which you put on your lance, generally. If you had one. Most knights had quite a big lance, which tended to be extremely popular with the ladies, while other knights had little lances and found it quite a problem finding a lady at all.

The Black Death, on the other hand, come from the fact that people chucked all their plate scrapings and buckets of everything into the streets or into the house opposite,[1] which wasn't difficult seeing as

---

[1] Including to be perfectly candid, their personal waste or 'toiletry' deposits, if you get my meaning, of which I need say no more, except that there would have been an appalling

fourteenth-century houses were generally only inches apart. Which means that everyone got everyone else's slops all the time. As they do in fact to this day in many modern Italian camp sites.

All in all, three people in every one died of the Black Death. At one point there wasn't anyone in Europe left at all. Just a load of empty countries and piles of dirty plates and sewage everywhere. If you was to imagine Hay-on-Wye on a Sunday morning, with half the sewage of Bombay piled up down the street, that was Europe at the time of the Black Death.

Witchcraft

The fourteenth century, of course, was famous for its witches, who were generally in charge of medieval community health care and were the equivalent to our modern-day local GP, although they were a bit harder to find, seeing as they generally lived in a fetid hovel in the middle of a dark forest with a couple of ravens or an owl. They continued more or less unabated until doctors were finally introduced by the National Health Service, which came in under Sir Thomas Beecham in 1948.

The fourteenth century was also famous for jousting, pilgrims, numerous popular tortures, Stephen and Matilda, acorns and steeple hats.

THINGS TO DO:

1. Fashion a noble and mighty sword from living steel, with a blade as true and straight as any in all England.

2. Choose from the following which popular medieval torture you would have chosen if you had had the choice:

    a. The Rack
    b. Iron Mask
    c. Pilliwinks
    d. The Brank
    e. Skeffington's Gyves
    f. Gondar's Newt
    g. Billington's Trousers.

3. Make your own steeple hat.

---

load, due to their massive families, owing to the total lack of birth control, except for the rhythm method and dock leaves.

CHAPTER XXXIII
THE NORMANS

'He is happiest who hath power
To gather wisdom from a flower.'

(Rasputin)

THE fourteenth century was generally Norman, in other words every-one was Norman normally, except of course for the Saxons who were Saxon. Naturally, most people preferred to be Norman seeing as you got a Motte and Bailey and a crest and were allowed to flog the Saxons, who were also your serfs and thus the equivalent of modern-day working-class people.

The Normans, of course, are famous for Norman Churches, the Battle of Hastings, rotating crops and their hair, which was the shortest the world had yet seen. Their main claim to fame however was, of course, the celebrated *Domesday Book*, which had everyone in England in it and was colossally big for this reason and took twenty-five oxen to drag it from town to town, so they could write everyone's name and address and hobbies down.

Despite its size, the *Domesday Book* was very popular, particularly at Christmas, when sales were astronomical. It swiftly went into paperback and became a world best-seller. The main problem with it, of course, was that no sooner was it published than it was out of date, particularly with regard to the Saxons, who were permanently escalating the population after dark in their hovels.

It is a well-known fact that the population of America rose by 29 million after a half-hour power failure in New York City in 1953. So when we realize that the Saxons lived in a permanent power failure throughout their lives and had nothing else to do after the sun went down *apart* from escalate the population, we can begin to see why the authors of the

Domesday Book got so depressed and regularly committed suicide.

For this reason, the authors of many modern guides and directories must live in the same state of permanent despair. The authors of many telephone directories, for example. Or Mr Leslie Halliwell, author of the famous *Halliwell's Film Guide*, which is a kind of twentieth century *Domesday Book of Films*, and who must hear the news of each new film release as just one more nail in his coffin.[1]

LITTLE-KNOWN FACTS NO. 2

One fascinating little-known fact about the Normans is that they were not in fact Normans, but *French*! And came originally from Calais, Dieppe and Boulogne, which are three of the most desolate towns the world has ever known, so it is not surprising that they moved to England under the major Norman, William, who was also called the Conqueror, seeing as he beat Harold Nicholson at Hastings, the attractive family resort on the south coast. After him come William II, William III, William IV, William V, William Rufus, William and Mary, and William of Orange, all of whom continued the Norman conquest to the four corners of the world. It is not certain exactly how far they got but there is a Hastings in Nebraska and one in Michigan and, most amazing of all, one in New Zealand. As well as a New Brighton and a Nelson, which is pretty conclusive evidence that the Normans invaded there too.

It is also my surmise that the celebrated stone gods on Aku Aku, the famous Easter Island are in fact wearing Norman helmets and are none other than replicas of Norman monarchs. At the same time, it must also be more than mere coincidence that *both* the Normans *and* the Americans have Sheriffs.

There are also Sheriffs in Arabia, of course, who are high-up Sheikhs. They still exist to this day and one of the most famous, of course, is the world famous actor Omar Sharif, as his name implies. I have as it happens

---

[1] I would just like to say, at this juncture, that I have read Mr Halliwell's book from cover to cover and while I recognise the many hours he must have put in, I would like to know how he can say, and I quote, that '*The Ten Commandments* is incredibly stilted and verbose . . . a very long haul along a monotonous route with the director at his pedestrian worst' when it is a well-known fact that *The Ten Commandments* is one of the greatest, most moving and most spiritually important films ever made. Or how he can just write off *Genghis Khan* which, after all, starred not only Omar Sharif but also Robert Morley and JAMES MASON, as a 'meandering epic in which brutality alternates with pantomimish comedy and bouts of sex!' And *how* Mr Halliwell can describe *Ben Hur*, which is the *the* greatest film ever made by anybody as 'surprisingly unimaginative' is totally beyond me! In fact I would like to ask Mr Halliwell to view these masterpieces once again before permitting another edition of this volume to enter the public sector.

had the privilege of meeting Mr Sharif in the 'wings', as we call them, of the Theatre Royal, Drury Lane, just before 'going on' (another theatrical expression) to appear at the world famous SWET Awards Ceremony, which is certainly the glittering pinnacle in the entire theatrical calendar and one that no-one in 'The Profession' would dare to miss. The Wimbledon, if you will, of world theatre. In fact I took the opportunity of personally congratulating Mr Sharif on his performance in *Lawrence of Arabia* and in fact suggested a couple of minor character details that might possibly have improved his performance slightly. I also took the opportunity of availing him of a couple of little chess moves that I thought might be of interest.

His apparent aloofness was probably little more than a chronic attack of nerves which many foreign actors get before an appearance on the English stage. Hardly surprising when we recall that Great Britain is of course the mother of all theatre. Like she is the mother of all parliaments and mother of most other things, in fact.

One of the most famous Norman events, of course, was the Magna Carta which was done by King John at Runnymede owing to the Peasant's Revolt. John, of course, was a well-known inadequate who wasn't supposed to be King, whereas Richard the Lionheart, who was an early version of Henry V, *was*, but went to fight the Crusades and got arrested as soon as he got off the boat for customs offences. For this reason, England went to the dogs and Richard languished in a Turkish prison until he got rescued by Blondel, the famous tight-rope-walker and escapologist, who not only crossed the Grand Canyon on a unicycle with seven novice monks on his head, but also escaped from a suit of armour in a Turkish coffin embedded in twenty feet of concrete at the bottom of the Vistula.

Richard came straight back to England, deposed John, then died of the Black Death, so John took over again until he died in the Wash. In fact, ninety per cent of all Norman Kings died.

Obviously, not all the Normans was cruel or weak. Some Normans were heroic men, similar to men of our own time like Douglas Bader or Edith Cavell. These were Henry V, chiefly, who beat the pathetic and weak French under their corrupt and decadent King Dauphin who had tragically thin legs and black tights and was like a very thin version of Richard III without the hunch. He was very cruel to his people and is famous for burning Joan of Arc, due to her voices.

In fact all French monarchs are famous for their cruelty and decadence, especially Louis XIV the famous sun king and Marie Antoinette his wife, a jumped-up interior decorator from Rheims, who fell under the influence of the sinister Archbishop Makarios and spent the entire French budget on mirrors and dressing-tables. They then tragically alienated the French peasantry by dressing up as simulated shepherds and frolicking about with the French nobility who wore wigs and beauty spots and spent their time running the peasants over in their carriages. For this reason the peasants rose with their pitchforks, invented the guillotine and killed everyone with a wig or a beauty spot, which wasn't particularly surprising but was a little hard on people with toupees and moles, obviously.

This period is known as the French Revolution, and is remembered chiefly, of course, for the Scarlet Pimpernel, who was actually an Englishman and whose memory lives on in the legendary English flower that was named after him. It is small and red, as was he. He dressed up as old women and railway porters and his daring exploits often involved the aristocracy dressing up as old women and railway porters too. This many of them refused to do, because old women's and railway porters' clothes tended to be very smelly.

His numbers did increase massively, however, when he managed to smuggle some specially perfumed old women's and porters' outfits into France. Although the French *douaniers* or customs officials,[1] being revolutionaries, soon got wise to this exodus of sweet-scented old women and porters flooding through Calais.

From now on all old women and porters were guillotined regardless of their political affiliations or how they smelt.

The Scarlet Pimpernel leading the disguised French Aristocracy through customs

[1] Under their leader, the dreaded primitive artist, Douanier Rousseau.

CHAPTER XXXIV
MODERN FRANCE

'Can this cockpit hold the vasty fields of France.'

(Squadron Leader Guy Gibson)

AFTER the French Revolution, the French coat–of–arms was changed to a woman standing in the wind and, to this day, France is a changed nation and everybody is very happy.

Apart from that, nothing has happened in French history of any major significance, except the Eiffel Tower, *The French Lieutenant's Woman* and French Windows,[1] but this we shouldn't hold against them. In fact I would like to say that all the French people I know are all very nice indeed – unlike a few *other* continental folk I could mention. The only French people, in fact, who, in my estimation, leave anything to be desired at all are certain members of the catering staff on French cross-channel ferries, some of whom were unnecessarily rude to Wallace and myself, when we requested vegeetarian meals on a recent cultural day-trip to the famous hypermarket at Dunkirk, whose cheese counter alone is approximately a mile and a half long.

I am, of course, a vegetarian for spiritual and moral reasons while Wallace is a vegetarian due to the fact that he throws up when he sees meat. But, whatever our reasons, there was no need for what I can only describe as *some of the most unnecessary and personal harassment that has probably ever been seen in the entire history of maritime catering.*

THINGS TO DO:

1. Travel by Sealink *British* Ferries.

---

[1] French Windows have revolutionized the modern living-room throughout the world – seeing as without them it would still be virtually impossible to step straight on to our patio or lawns.

CHAPTER XXXV
A HISTORY OF THE ENGLISH CHANNEL

'They are never alone that are accompanied by noble thoughts.'

(Sir Philip Sidney)

OVER the millennia, the English Channel has been crossed by numerous forms of historic shipping.

But probably the most famous and certainly the best in my opinion without any shadow of a doubt is Sealink British Car Ferries.

With spanking new interior décor, fully refurbished restaurant facilities and on-board videos for the kiddies, Sealink British believe your holiday starts the moment you step aboard.

There's also a cheerful on-deck refreshment service and bags of room for your hand luggage! Yes – Sealink British will turn your Crossing into a Cruise.

Anyhow, probably the most famous thing done by the Normans was the Crusades which in fact occurred next, as a matter of interest, and was between us and the Arabs.[1]

---

[1] I am of course fully aware that I have slightly strayed from the strictly chronological at this juncture. Needless to say, this is entirely intentional and *isn't* because 'I'm losing my grip' actually, Wallace. It is in fact an example of what is technically known as a 'tangent' and is what many leading authors go off at in order to make numerous crucial points that they *couldn't have made* if they hadn't gone off at it. In fact many books would make no sense at all if it wasn't for tangents. As a matter of interest it is generally agreed that tangents are probably the single most important ingredient in the modern novel today. In fact I happen to know that Sir Geoffrey Methuen, who probably knows more about the art of writing than many people, is very keen on tangents and has recently sent out a memo throughout the literary world requesting a greater use of tangents generally.

CHAPTER XXXVI
THE CRUSADES

'Any fool can criticize and most fools do.'

(Celestial Seasonings Herb Teas)

THE Crusades, in fact, lasted for six hundred years and was fought over *Constantinople*, which was in fact *Rome* until it was re-named Constantinople so as to avoid capture. For this reason it kept moving about, which is why the war[1] went on for so long because nobody knew where it was at any given time.

It did, however, give the Pope a chance to clear up the streets of Rome and shift all the broken pillars and rotting fruit and so forth so as he could get Roman Catholicism off the ground. This street clearance or 'Rome Improvement' as it became known, was mainly done by the Swiss Guard who wear short skirts and pom-poms, but are extremely clean, like all Swiss people. Not as clean as the Swedes, obviously, but still very hygienic. No doubt the holy Pontiff would have had the Swedes in, except they was still Vikings and therefore pagan.

In fact due to the appalling paganism still going on everywhere, the Pope sent out numerous well-known saints such as St Patrick, St Augustus, St Benedictine and St Bruno to combat the endless heathens who still believed in corn dollies and curing boils with dandelions and so forth.

To aid them in their tasks, of course, many of the saints were allowed to perform miracles, which must have come in very handy if you was doing a conversion, particularly of an entire pagan people. St Patrick, for instance, rid Ireland of snakes and as a result thousands of great hairy lager-swilling

---

[1] Also known as the Wars of the Roses, the Hundred Years War and the War of the Worlds.

THE CRUSADES

Some Famous Saints

| St Augustus | St Patrick | St Benedictine | St Bruno |

Vikings became devout church-goers overnight,[1] which is hardly surprising when you think about it. In other words, if a Moonie came to my house and I had a plague of black mamba in the garden and he got rid of them all, *I'd* be a Moonie.

That's not true, of course, seeing as I am a Zen Buddhist. I'm simply making a psychological observation with regard to human behavioural processes.

And so it was that the sun set on the mighty Norman Empire – without which the world would have been a very different place indeed, needless to say.

THINGS TO DO:

1. There are still many Norman names in the world today. Examples are Norman Fowler, Norman St John Stevens and Norman Tebbit. See how many more you can discover.

2. Make a scale model of a rotating crop.

3. Write short notes on the following: a) dandelions; b) Archbishop Makarios; c) Hastings; d) Weston-Super-Mare.

---

[1] As a result, St Patrick received offers from many other countries, such as India, Australia and South America who offered sole and unconditional conversion rights in repayment for the total abolition of all snakes, spiders, piranhas etc. Patrick, however, would never leave his native Ireland, which is why these countries are so appallingly full of deadly snakes and fish.

CHAPTER XXXVII
THE STORY OF ST FRANCIS

'Fair stood the wind for Francis.'

(Anon)

PROBABLY the most internationally renowned saint, however, was St
Francis of Assisi, who was the rich son of a medieval cloth merchant
who one day give all his father's cloth to beggars, which didn't please his
father, obviously. Or indeed the beggars. Who now had to wander the
plague-infested back streets of Renaissance Italy with their prams not only
full of old newspapers and fire-grates but also thundering great twenty-foot
bales of heavy curtain material.

For this reason, St Francis was publicly beaten by his father, so he cut a
tonsure on his head and went about the land preaching to all the animals.
And the animals stopped whatever they was doing, and sat by St Francis
and quietly listened to him. And the birds, too, and the fishes. And even the
trees also. And as a result of having heard his words, the birds sang in the air
and the fish sang in the sea and the flowers sang in their fields and the moles
sang in their burrows.

The Famous Wolf of Gubbio Story
And a wolf was killing sheep and terrifying the attractive Italian village of
Gubbio which was trying to destroy it and thus advertising for a knight. So
St Francis came and said 'I will go.' So he went. And they said, 'Take with
you a sword'; and he said 'No.' And he went in his habit and his tonsure and
he found the wolf in his lair and the wolf was snarling but Francis went in.

And the people waited behind their walls and Francis did not return
and the red sun was just sinking below the Umbrian hills when they spied
through the olive groves a man walking with a wolf wagging his tail. (The
wolf wagging his tail, obviously, not Francis.) And the wolf lay at his feet

and let them stroke him and the people let him lick their hand and the wolf stayed in the village and became their friend, and St Francis said, 'There is no need for fear no more.'

And he went up a hill and became older than he'd ever been or would ever be again and saw a six-winged Seraph[1] and immediately understood everything as clear as a bell and saw to the bottom of the depths of all infinity, and stood on the head of a pin and saw the universe in a raindrop, and totally knew the answer to every question that had ever been asked. And he saw life as a tiny little closed potting shed inside a wondrous eternal garden. And realized that all human anxiety was but a single pebble in the ocean.

The End of Francis
And he lay there for six days and for six nights and was nearly frozen solid and the monks come and took him home and he sang and smiled and said 'I have been there, sunshine.' And just before he died they got him a load of blankets and ermine and hot-water bottles and a jewelled fur hat and so on because his body shivered greatly. And they also got him a load of biscuits and buns and cakes as a last treat, because they loved him.

But St Francis said, 'No, no, carry me and put me on the cold night earth without any clothes or cakes or buns or anything. Put me beneath the stars into the hearts of which I have journeyed when I was up the hill.' So they placed him naked on the naked ground and they stood with him and watched. And little animals crept up too and watched also. And owls. And the wolf. And they all said goodbye.

And that was the story of Francis of Assisi.

THINGS TO DO:

1. See if there is a nearby town or village where an untamed pet is dangerously rampant from lack of self-esteem. Go there, unarmed, and talk to the animal.

2. Build the Doge of Venice.

[1] Six-winged Seraph = an extremely high-up angel with six wings.

CHAPTER XXXVIII

THE ARAB EMPIRE

'All the perfumes of Arabia
will not sweeten this little hand.
Oh! Oh! Oh!'

(William Shakespeare)

SO it was that the world of the fourteenth century was chiefly governed by the Normans who – as we have seen – was in fact not Norman but English. With English Kings, like Edward the Professor, English buildings like the Bank of England and English customs like maypole dancing, shove ha'penny and apple bobbing. In other words, it can safely be said that the world, in most respects, was ruled by England.

Then – suddenly – nearly the whole world started being taken over by the Arabs, which was a terrible shock, to say the least, seeing as the Arabs normally just live a very quiet nomadic life in their tents, herding goats and playing dice and not saying a word to anybody unless they have to. Or so everyone thought.

One can imagine, therefore, the utter dismay of world leaders and the world generally when they all started pounding out of Saudi Arabia on their racing camels and just started taking over nearly everywhere.

They appeared from nowhere like burning shadows flying through the blood-red rays of the setting sun with their long robes and curly daggers and their wild eyes like liquid pools of black fire gleaming behind their yashmaks. There was, in fact, one Norman Foreign Legion outpost in a small fort in Tangiers where men had come to find their souls, to lose their pasts, to escape their fate and face their fear, where no questions were asked and no mercy given, where boys became men and men became animals. But they put up only token resistance and were defeated in three minutes.

The Arabs then immediately swept across the world and conquered it within a week.

THE ARAB EMPIRE

Now it would be stupid to deny that the Arabs have occasionally tended to be rather a, shall we say, less than merciful race at times during their history and even today – *very occasionally* – do still have the odd public mass execution and so forth. However, I think it is very important to point out at this juncture that the Arabian people have nowadays almost completely turned over a new leaf and put all that behind them. In fact it is my personal opinion that they are now amongst the most merciful people on the whole earth and will always welcome you into their tent where they still live to this day, despite their fabulous wealth beyond even Ali Baba or John Paul Getty II.[1]

---

[1] John Paul Getty II, the well-known millionaire is often confused with Pope John Paul II, the current Pope. Although only in regard to the uncanny similarity of their names, it goes without saying. In other words, while John Paul Getty II is unbelievably wealthy and has gold bath taps and has bought all his grandchildren miniature Bentleys, Pope John Paul II is not wealthy at all. (He wears jewels and so on on his cassock of course and the rubies on his mitre alone are worth more than seven Arab oil wells, as he would be the first to admit, but these are all the property of the Vatican, obviously, and not his *personally*, it goes without saying. The Pope in fact does not actually live in the Vatican at all but in a medieval daub-and-wattle hut at the back. While his private apartment in the Papal jet is hung with old sacking and over-run with chickens.) I would just like to say at this point that while I have never actually met Mr Getty, I believe, having just thought about it, that he and the Pope probably *do* in fact share more than their names and that, like the Pope, Mr Getty is probably a very deeply spiritual person indeed. My reason for suggesting this is that I have recently heard that Mr Getty sometimes chooses to enrich the world of culture by buying famous paintings for the National Gallery and so on. I have also been profoundly moved to hear that he personally donates private funding to individual creative artists. Thus enabling them to write or paint and so forth while keeping the wolf from the door, as it were. At the same time giving them the confidence that for the rest of their creative days they will never ever again have to face the harrowing effects of financial destitution. This is obviously the vision of a man who cares deeply for the arts and indeed for all human beings on earth. In fact it is my belief that his massive generosity towards artists, in whose illustrious company I would presume, with humility yet with pride, to include myself, will make the world a richer place to live in, if you get my meaning, and if Mr Getty feels, on reading this little volume (a mere bauble, I have no doubt, compared to the many leather-clad first editions of Galileo, Aristotle, Bernard Russell and the like that must adorn his libraries across the world, but one that is, perhaps, worthy in its own unpretentious way) that he might be able to assist my own artistic endeavours in any way, financially or otherwise – although financially would be most useful, obviously (a standing order, perhaps, or perhaps the guaranteed monthly payment of all domestic bills or income tax, possibly; or perhaps if Mr Getty has any country properties in, say, Sussex or overlooking Windermere or even further afield like the South of France, near the sea if possible with a garden not too close to the main road, that he would like regularly looked after by an artist or would even like to in fact purchase *for* an artist such as myself) then perhaps Mr Getty would care to contact me any time at his convenience:
c/o Sir Geoffrey Methuen,
The Penthouse,
Methuen Books Ltd.,
New Fetter Lane,
London E1A DE0.

And so it was that the mighty Arab Empire came to an end. Probably the greatest empire the world has ever known. Apart from the British obviously, as I'm sure the Arabs would be the first to agree.

THINGS TO DO:

1. Paint an Arabian Knight.

CHAPTER XXXIX
THE RENAISSANCE

'The next major thing that occurred after the Normans was the Renaissance, as is well known.'

(D. Dingle)

AND so it was that, after the Arabs, the next major thing to occur was the Renaissance. The reason it was called the Renaissance, of course, was all the famous statues, buildings and music, which was done at the time, such as the 'Mona Lisa', *Wuthering Heights* and Mozart's 'Moonlight Sonata', without whom the world would never be the same again and were chiefly the result of Queen Elizabeth I, who started the Renaissance off single-handed, so to speak, and is therefore the most famous monarch of all time, as is our own Queen today, obviously.

For this reason the Renaissance is popularly known across the world as the Elizabethan Age or the Age of Elizabeth. Unfortunately, Queen Elizabeth I – unlike our own Queen, who clearly delights in her joint role as housewife and monarch – never married or sired an heir. Not, obviously, because she wasn't a very attractive woman which she clearly was (maybe not everyone's cup of tea but certainly nothing out of place, if you get my meaning) but so as she could devote her entire life to patronising the arts and go on tour with various theatre companies.

It is ironic that Elizabeth I came closest to marriage when she met the suave, charming and recklessly good-looking Philip II of Spain (*see* plate 7d). After going out with him for a few years, she finally chose to put the Renaissance before her animal urges, but if she hadn't and had married him, then *her* husband would have been called Philip too, exactly like our own Queen's is. A fascinating coincidence of history that didn't come to pass but could have.

The most famous name, however, given to this epoch is, of course, the

The Mona Lisa – the famed painting by Leonardo da Vinci. The Anaconda Smile has mystified and intrigued art-lovers for centuries. Stand this open page on the mantelpiece and observe how she follows you about the room.

Golden Age of Shakespeare who, as I explained earlier, is without doubt the most famous person the world has ever known.

I'm afraid it has to be said, however, that despite this universally acknowledged *fact*, there are still *certain* countries who insist on calling the Renaissance the Age of one of their own so-called artists. Not that it matters what you call an age, obviously. It's what happens in the age that is important, as I would be the first to agree, but I do feel it is only fair to apportion credit where it is rightly due, particularly in the case of Shakespeare. However, Inappropriate Age-Naming (as it is known technically) *does* still go on in many countries and I think it only right to mention it at this juncture.

In Italy, for instance, the Golden Age of Shakespeare is known as the Golden Age of Botticelli; in Spain the Golden Age of El Cid; in Holland the Golden Age of Delft; in Russia the Golden Age of Chekhov; and so on. Now fair enough, if you are referring to a couple of years in your own country's history. Maybe *two* or *three* years of Italian history could be called the Golden Age of Botticelli. I would not for a minute wish to deny him his glory. He knew a fair deal about painting and his Venus de Milo is one of the best nudes ever done, as any art expert will tell you. He is also the name of a world-famous adult game, played to this day at fashionable parties, often with tragic consequences. But to call the whole Renaissance the Golden Age of Botticelli is ridiculous and absurd.

It is not that other countries refuse to recognise Shakespeare's greatness. A quick glance at the audience at the Royal Stratford Theatre on Avon will tell you that! Where every third person wears a kimono or a fez and the only English you will hear all night is *on stage*. It is quite simply that other countries are absurdly partisan and jingoistic about having one of their own artists as the person whose Golden Age it is – which would be fine *if* they had done as much or more than we did in the Renaissance. But they didn't.

It was a prolific time, I grant you, when art burst like a mighty iridescent sun through the clouds of the Black Death; but even so, each country only really had the *one* art form they was good at, while we just happened to be blessed with many. Obviously no-one's blaming them for not having more, but that's just the way it was. And still is, as it happens, but that's another story. Anyway, in my view, other countries should just stop complaining and learn to accept it and be grateful that they have an art-form at all. Unlike some countries I could mention, like Belgium, Iceland or Canada,[1] for example, who have none.

All pretty conclusive proof, anyway, that England was not only the world-leader, but also the inspiration, the *Maison d'être*, if you will, of the Renaissance, and without whom, probably, the whole Renaissance would have just petered out after one or two years.

Breakthroughs in Art

The Renaissance was also responsible for numerous breakthroughs in art. One of the most famous breakthroughs, in some cases literally, was the art of perspective, in which artists done paintings of distance that were so realistic that people felt you could walk into them. In fact many Renaissance paintings were ruined because members of the public kept walking straight through them and out the other side, thinking it was in fact a real landscaped garden or canal.

This is why many art galleries introduced the brass-knobbed posts and white rope barriers that are still in use to this day. They have also been introduced into many banks, building societies and Post Offices, as it happens, although, of course, this has nothing to do with the art of perspective, obviously, but the parlous state of present-day queueing which unfortunately is not what it used to be, since we opened our ports to all and sundry tourists, who just start pushing in willy-nilly the moment they see a cashier.

---

[1] While I have the attention of Canadian readers, I would just like to say 'howdy' to the many new Canadian friends that I will have made as a result of this work and to openly admit, that up until now (and extraordinarily for someone who has traversed the globe probably more times than Lope de Vega), the kingdom of Canada has not been a country I have yet had the honour of visiting. Needless to say, this is solely due to my ever-increasing commitments as an author and world celebrity and has nothing whatsoever to do with the fact that Canada is seen, by some, as rather a backwater (let us not mince words) on the mighty stage of the international spectrum. However, I would just like to say that, despite this, I have always felt a massive and profound affinity with all Canadian peoples who, of course, originated in England anyway and whose country is so uncannily like our own. Having its own Lake District, Pennines and numerous famed cities, such as Toronto and Quebec, modelled, as they are, on the classic British cities, such as Leicester and Grantham (*see* comparative photos on plate seven). Anyway, Wallace and myself would just like to mention that we certainly look forward to our very first cultural tour of the famed and fabulous 'Realm of Eternal Winter' (and would be available for this purpose any time at their convenience).

Not every country, obviously. The Swiss, for instance, never push in willy-nilly; neither do the Danes, who are some of the most polite people in queues I have ever had the privilege of meeting. No, I am referring (without naming any names obviously) to some of the more, shall we say, latin-blooded countries who have been known to turn many a quiet little half-timbered bank in the Cotswolds into a personal hell for numerous British holiday-makers.

The Male Nude

Another breakthrough was the male nude. Before the Renaissance no-one painted men nude. They painted women nude, obviously, but not men and if they did paint men nude they was covered by a leaf or vine. Suddenly, however, Renaissance painters and decorators just started showing men totally naked with nothing on. For this reason many people, mainly women, but also some men who had never dared look, were deeply shocked and fainted when they saw these male nudes, seeing as they often didn't know that what men have there is there, thinking that men have leaves or vines permanently where they in fact have their parts.

Nowadays, of course, we see a statue of a naked man with all his parts showing and no-one bats an eyelid but in those days a man showing all his parts even in stone or marble was a deeply shocking experience and many people went around after the Renaissance adding leaves or knocking bits off. This was called the Reformation.

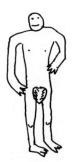

The Male Nude during the Renaissance

W: *And wasn't astronomy another major invention of the Elizabethan or Shakespearian age?*

It certainly was, Wallace. Astronomy was indeed another major invention of the Elizabethan or Shakespearian Age. And numerous astronomers come to fruition at this time, the most famous of whom being Galileo who had a beard and invented the telescope via which he discovered that the earth goes round the sun. Which meant of course, that the sun didn't go round the earth, as was thought previous. Unfortunately, this was not warmly received by the Pope, who had already sent out a massive bull which went about telling everybody that the earth was the centre of the Universe and that he definitely *knew* this, seeing as he was Pope. Which meant that if someone proved it *wasn't* the centre of the Universe, he was a ruined man, with nothing but a massive wife, thirty screaming children, half a dozen chickens and a rat-infested hovel in the windswept outskirts of Livorno to look forward to. In other words, being a defrocked Pope in the Renaissance was no laughing matter. And certainly didn't mean a retirement villa and life pension on the holiday Isle of Capri, which it does for defrocked Popes nowadays, of course.

So it was that on 1st October 1621, the Pope asked Galileo round for a drink and showed him a machine that sucks your innards out of your nose for thirty-six days while you are buried up to your neck in a flesh-eating ant-hill.

The following morning Galileo discovered that the sun *does* in fact go round the earth, which was therefore – as had been thought originally – the Centre of the Universe. He apologized for his error and admitted that he thought it was the sun he saw through the telescope with all the planets whizzing round it, whereas in fact it wasn't the sun, obviously, it was the earth he had seen which looked remarkably similar on that particular day.

W: *So was there any other advances made at this time?*

Yes, Wallace, there was numerous advances in Medicine.

Advances in Medicine

Meanwhile there was numerous advances in medicine. Particularly in England where Sir Harvey Nicholls had just invented Surgery which soon caught the imagination of the entire medical profession. So much so that enthusiastic young doctors began doing it on anyone regardless of the ailment. Dysentery, hay fever, influenza, depression. Anything was slapped on the operating table.

To begin with, Health Clinics were crammed with patients eager to go beneath the surgeon's scalpel but interest tailed off sharply after only a few weeks when it was discovered that nobody had yet invented anaesthetics.[1]

W: *So was there any other famous Renaissance doctors and nurses?*

Yes, there certainly was, Wallace.

---

[1] The only form of anaesthetics in the Renaissance was of course the Renaissance bullet which they gave to patients to bite during the operation. The skill lay in seeing when the writhing patient had bitten *through* the bullet and inserting another bullet before the patient bit through his own jaw and often the operating table itself. Many anaesthetists lost fingers as a result and thus their whole livelihoods. Employment offices of the time were often crowded with tragic queues of white-coated fingerless Elizabethan anaesthetists.

Other Famous Renaissance Doctors and Nurses

Other famous Renaissance doctors and nurses, of course, were Florence Nightingale, Doctor Spock, Doctor Dolittle and Ian Fleming.

W: *And what about Michelangelo?*

One of the most famous artists of the time was, of course, Michelangelo, whose most famous work was the Sistine Chapel, and the nude statue of Moses, which he also done.

LITTLE KNOWN FACTS No. 3

Very few people know that Michelangelo was, in fact, born and bred a mere five minutes from the centre of Bournemouth (*see* plate 4). His parents left England when he was three to avoid the Black Death and went to Italy which is probably the worst place they could have gone, having probably the worst sanitation of anywhere in Europe, as it still does to this day. Though they couldn't have known that at the time, obviously.

As well as his great works of art, Michelangelo is also celebrated for the amount of self-loathing he achieved which was basically because he engaged in certain proclivities known nowadays as the Love That Dare Not Speak Its Name. I think I make myself clear. He did not care for the company of women, in other words. In fact, he loathed himself so much on this account that he forced himself to lie on his back day in day out wearing only a loin cloth and paint the Creation. It is hard to believe that the man who done this wouldn't even look in a mirror, so much did he loathe himself on account of his proclivities which are nowadays quite normal and is the choice of many people, many of whom are famous in all walks of life.

Michelangelo was, of course, played by Charlton Heston in the famous film *The Agony and the Ecstasy*. And superbly too, if I may say so. Needless to say, Mr Heston has never had to engage in the Love That Dare Not Speak Its Name and has a charming wife, a red setter and two delightful children, Frazer and Holly.

THINGS TO DO:

1. Discuss why it was you think the Renaissance died out so suddenly. Was it a) disease b) drought c) climatic catastrophe d) the critics?

2. Write short notes on the following Renaissance subjects:
a) *Wuthering Heights*; b) the Cotswolds; c) Dysentery; d) Iceland;
e) *El Cid* (which also starred Charlton Heston, of course, and
who, in my personal view, is the world's greatest actor bar Sir
Laurence Olivier, with whom he in fact appeared to play the
title role in the legendary British film *Khartoum*).

3. See *Khartoum*.

CHAPTER XL
THE LIFE OF THE BUDDHA

'I am The Buddha.'

(Buddha)

BUDDHA was a very rich Indian prince who had everything his heart could desire. Fine clothes and turbans, jewels and peacocks, gold howdahs, tandoori cooking and a very rare pet Muntjac deer. But one day his eye fell upon all the suffering people of India who were just wandering about in pain outside the palace walls. Some were in silent twos and threes, many were alone. A few sat on the hard, shadeless mud surrounded by flies and being picked off by snakes, but most just walked around crying to themselves and wondering why they weren't dead.

And so, despite his parents' entreaties, he left the jewel-encrusted palace and walked the dusty roads of India on his horse. And after seeing all the suffering in the entire world he sat under a fig tree and meditated for seventy-five years and his jewellery and ear-rings and ankle-chains and everything but his loin-cloth fell off and lay about him where he sat, and his very expensive horse hung about waiting to go, got thin and died suddenly under its jewelled saddle, and all the figs withered and everything decayed and disintegrated around him, until he was just sat there on his own in his loin-cloth which hadn't disintegrated, fortunately, and birds came and nested in his hair, seeing as they thought he was a bush.

And Buddha, having been sat under this tree for seventy-five years, discovered what it takes a practising Zen Buddhist nowadays of course, such as myself, a mere weekend to grasp. Basically that:

a) We must totally *rid ourselves of our egos* which – after many years of constant meditational practice (*see* photographic sequence a–f, plate 8: The Desmond Dingle Guide to Buddhist Meditation) – I

114

have totally succeeded in doing, I'm very happy to say. In fact I now have virtually no ego left whatsoever.[1]

and:

b) That we are free of all pain and nothing can hurt us seeing as everything doesn't exist anyway so we don't exist, because there isn't anything anyway, seeing as it's all illusion and this is basically the answer to all suffering as we know it today. And one which I have personally found very helpful in my own life which has not exactly been devoid of pain to put it mildly.[2]

[1] In fact a number of well-known Buddhist monks have actually told me that, of all the people they've known who've done meditation, I have, without a doubt, in their opinion, reached deeper levels of spiritual awareness than probably anybody else doing it today.

[2] Obviously, I am a very successful historian, classical actor and philosopher as well as a psychoanalyst, television presenter and religious expert. But I would be lying if I said that I hadn't had my share of suffering – like many major artists. And I'm not just talking about the trivial problems of domestic life, neither, like blocked sinks or washing-machines breaking down. I am talking about very dark, personal and profound *pain*, born in some of the deepest recesses of the human soul. Although my washing-machine *has* actually broken down, as a matter of interest. In fact, it has broken down *constantly* ever since I bought it a *mere three months ago* – if you can believe that! I admit that I am probably partly to blame seeing as I made the mistake of purchasing this item from a Discount House, as I believe they are called. The mistake being, of course, that there is *no service agreement* on the sales contract, owing to the discounted price on the product. This means that while your original outlay is reasonable you pay through the nose each time it goes wrong, which appears to be every five days if our machine is anything to go by. Granted, the first time was due to the fact that I foolishly allowed myself to be misled by Wallace, who convinced me that it is possible to wash a seventeen-foot square goatskin rug in a six-pound drum, if you can believe that. And possibly I *have* tended to rather overload it at times, due to the fact that I have an extremely artistic temperament and, dealing as I do with very deep human and complex historical issues, can hardly be doing with irritating domestic con-cerns like running back and forth to check with the Easy Wash and Care Instruction Manual that I've got the *right* button pushed at the *right* time at the *right* temperature etc., etc., etc. Would Dr Jacob Bronowski – one of the greatest men who ever lived and one on whom I have modelled my entire life – have always remembered how many socks and underpants to put in his washing-machine before it went into overload and conked out? Of course not. He was busy pondering the nature of meaning under the anglepoise in his book-lined study. And rightly too. That was what he was put on the planet for. Not operating a washing-machine. He had a good lady wife who done that – Lady Bronowski, in fact – just as I have Wallace. Not – I hasten to add – that Wallace and I are married. It goes without saying, obviously, that neither Wallace nor myself have any abnormality in that respect. Not, I am sure that anyone would have suggested that we did, but just in case there is anyone who wishes to cast slurs, I would like to make it absolutely clear that Wallace and I are both perfectly normal with no aberrances in the Michelangelo depart-ment if you get my meaning. Not that there'd be anything wrong in it obviously if we had. As I have mentioned, many famous people choose this proclivity without batting an eyelid. It's just that we are not is what I'm saying and certainly never have been, thank you very much. What I meant, quite simply, was that I have an arrangement with Wallace, whereby he rents the lower maisonette in my dwelling in exchange for certain tasks of a domestic nature, such as running the washing-machine. Or *not* running it, if it doesn't work obviously.

And thus it was that Buddha invented Buddhism and helped the suffering of the world. Buddhists nowadays wear orange robes and have bald heads so as to deter birds when they meditate.

I would just like to say that as a result of a recent past-life regression hypnosis session, I now have evidence that I was once a very big Tibetan Llama which will explain how I know so much about this fascinating but complex subject.

THINGS TO DO:

1. Become one with the spontaneous non-duality of the moment outside of all ego-concentrated time limitations.

CHAPTER XLI
THE RENAISSANCE MAN

'A verray parfit Rennaysons mann
who donne numirous Rennaysons dedis.'

(Gilbert Chaucer – grand-nephew of Geoffrey Chaucer)

ONE crucial result of the Renaissance which has only recently come to my attention, otherwise I would have mentioned it earlier, and which I personally find very very interesting, was the famous concept of the Renaissance Man, which come to fruition at this time and who I would like to spend a few moments dwelling on, if I may, at this juncture.

The true Renaissance Man was expected to be able to collect art, write poetry, play a musical instrument, read and write Latin and Greek, speak several languages, fence, ride, be good at all sports, keep up with the fashions, show good manners to all, be popular with children, keep abreast of world news, be an expert on wines, know all the latest books, be an excellent conversationalist, have a profound affinity with the natural world, look good in tights, and be a practising Buddhist.

As we look about ourselves today, there are probably very few people we could think of who could fit this extremely demanding bill.

Readers, in fact, might like to compile their own lists. Don't forget your nominees must fit *all* categories. Here is my list. Compiled after considerable thought and research:

The Duke of Edinburgh
Omar Sharif
Magnus Magnusson
David Attenborough
Richard Attenborough
Sir Peter Hall

Desmond Olivier Dingle
Miriam Stoppard

Of course, I haven't seen any of the above gentlemen in tights, although *I* certainly have no problems in that particular area, nor, I'm quite certain, does Mrs Stoppard, who could look glamorous in a dustbin bag, in my opinion, and whose husband, if I may humbly proffer my own opinion at this point, is one of the greatest dramatists on the earth.

THINGS TO DO:

1. See Mr Stoppard's latest film *Amadeus*, which, although slightly tedious at certain points, if I may say so, held Wallace and I absolutely spellbound from start to finish. Four and a half hours of memorable cinema for £2 a head (Wallace and I generally go to the cinema on Mondays where our local Cannon offers matinee reductions on Mondays if you go in the afternoon) is remarkably good value in this day and age. Thank you Mr Stoppard. A great artist for all time!

I would just like to say, before closing this chapter, that I shall shortly be sending Mr Stoppard a number of my recent theatrical works for his comments. May I suggest that he too might like to send me some of his recent works for my comments, with a view to a possible collaboration and a real hit, I have no doubt, that could make us both quite a tidy sum?

CHAPTER XLII
OTHER MAJOR WORLD PHILOSOPHIES

'Groweth sed and bloweth med,
and springth the wude nu.'

(Unknown)

ANYWAY, besides Buddha, there was also numerous other major spiritual disciplines, such as Taoism, which is Chinese and teaches us to remember we are in tune with the sacred web of the universe and are no different to rivers or mountains or the innocent blades of grass. For instance, if you're an innocent blade of grass and the wind gently waves you and the sun warms you with its rays, you sit there and enjoy it, but if you're trodden on by a boot and crushed underfoot and then it drizzles and you die you have to lump it like any other blade of grass. Christianity is another famous philosophy, invented by Jesus, of course, and is very similar, as is Hinduism, invented by no-one in particular. All of them says basically the same thing: 'You are not here for why you think you are, you're here for another reason that we are not at liberty to tell you yet.'

THINGS TO DO:

1. Become a convert to a famous world religion.

CHAPTER XLIII
HISTORY IN THE HOME

'There are few things better, in my opinion,
than acting out a famous historic event in your
own garden or living-room.'

(Florence Nightingale)

AMONGST many other things, I am probably now most famous for my legendary re-enactments of history which have appeared of course on both stage and screen. As a result of these I have had literally sackfuls of letters from viewers writing to me personally, not only to thank me for having revived their interest in world culture, but also to ask me for various 'tips from the expert', as it were, on how to run their own historical re-enactments in their own homes.

For this reason I have decided to present – as part of this volume and for the first time in a work of such intellectual grandeur:-

★ A unique selection of suitable subjects for home re-enactment – *specially chosen by myself.*
★ A bevy of essential and time-saving hints for organizers that will give added enjoyment and educational value.
★ All historical details fully verified by my own specially trained historical authentication research unit.

9. SPARTACUS

The tyrant Crassus repels the gladiatorial hordes of rebel freedom fighters.

Although it is quite possible to re-enact most of the story in a normal self-contained flat or dwelling house, a garden is obviously essential for the bondage scenes in the salt mines and the mass crucifixions at the end. Ideal for all the family.

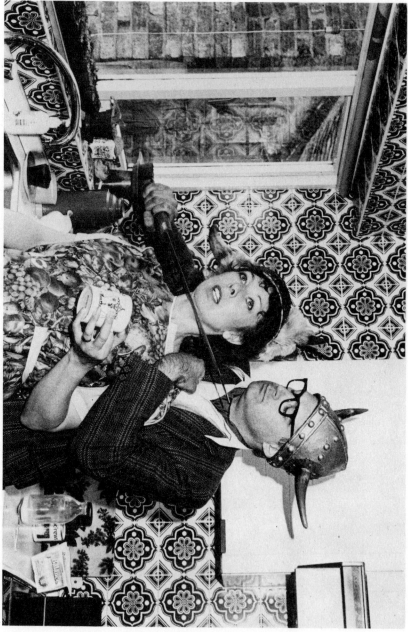

10. INVASION OF THE VIKINGS!

The gallant Britons defend their homesteads against the dreaded Norsemen. A good one for couples.
N.B. Check with your Insurance Company re additional premiums for battle re-enactments in the home. Don't
forget that actual burning and pillaging of property, particularly one's own, can be costly and upset neighbours. See
Plate 16 for a real-life example of tragic over-enthusiasm.

11. THE BATTLE OF BALACLAVA

The Heavy Brigade under legendary General Scarlett sweep down from the Fedioukine Heights to meet the crack Russian Dnieper Regiment on the windswept plains of Balaclava. The gallant Scots Greys (left) gallop to the rescue in perfect military formation. While the cruel and scheming Prince Menshikov and his generals (right) look on from the fourth Redoubt. Note the boldly imaginative use of numbers here.

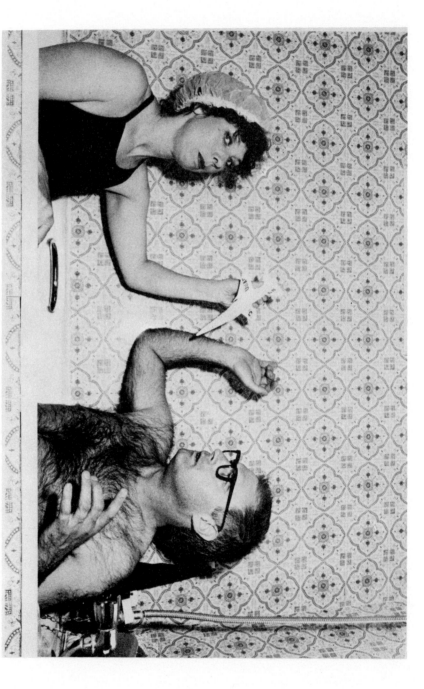

12. SINK THE BISMARCK!

Another excellent re-enactment for couples. Although, needless to say, **not** the very dubious so-called 'adult-game', common – so I hear – in certain Showbiz parties! **Our** "Sink the Bismarck" also happens to take place in the bath and is also played by two adult people but for no **other reason** than that the bathroom is the most appropriate setting for a naval battle. It would be naïve to suggest that this is a re-enactment for two total strangers but to try and fit more than two adults into the bath would be uncomfortable and upset the manoeuvering of the boats.

13. EXECUTION OF CHARLES I
Ideal for dwellings with limited accommodation.
Another good one for all the family and an
excellent introduction for friends.

*14a. Don't **always** go for the leading role! This organiser is in danger of losing the full attention of other participants.*

*14b. Allot roles with sensitive regard to age and agility.
This elderly person certainly has the maturity and no doubt the
acting skills to essay the demanding emotional range of Boadicea,
but it is unfair to expect her to participate in the strenuous battles, marches and
blood-letting rituals that the role necessitates.*

15a. Don't be TOO rigid with regard to total historical truth. **Be flexible!**
Let the Black Prince stand in front of the archers if he wants to.

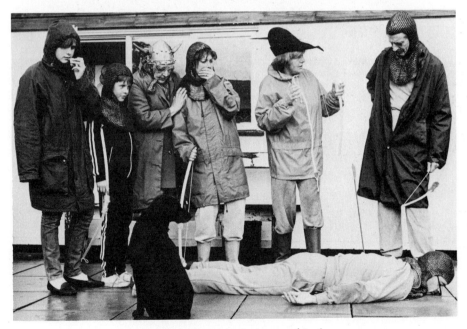

15b. Authenticity isn't everything!

16. WARNING

Be careful! This was the scene after Mr and Mrs Wearn of Epsom had attempted their own re-enactment of World War II. A little bit of care and forethought can save years of subsequent heartache. The Wearns' bill came to £203,000. Mr Wearn lost his job as a Consultant Rot Specialist, Mrs Wearn is in a home and the children, aged 8 and 11, a little boy and girl, are in Council care. History in the Home re-enactments bring families together, not rend them apart!

CHAPTER XLIV
THE BRITISH COMMONWEALTH

'This semi-precious gem,
This infectious bread of Kings.'

(Shakespeare)

AFTER the Elizabethan Age came the Puritans under Oliver Cromwell, who was a Roundhead. Meanwhile Elizabeth's heir, Charles I, was King and led the Cavaliers. Hence they had the Civil War. The reason being was the Roundheads was very stern and wore armour in the house and recycled their waste, while the Cavaliers had long hair, swaggered about and generally chucked everything away regardless.

The Situation Becomes Rapidly Untenable
For this reason, the situation became rapidly untenable and finally reached breaking point when a group of long-haired Cavaliers started swaggering on a Roundhead's recycled sprouts. There was a furore in the Commons and the following day the Civil War was declared, sweeping through Europe in a matter of weeks.

War Breaks Out
Immediately, the Roundheads turned their pitchforks into plowshares and marched on Buckingham Palace, which they razed to the ground, although the Cavaliers had all gone to Balmoral.

Peace Declared
After numerous battles at Edgware Road, Bunkers Hill and Bannockburn, the war came to an end when the Roundheads (or 'Johnny Reb') finally

captured the King – in disguise and totally bald – hiding up an oak tree, where he was immediately executed via beheading.

The Birth of Parliament

Oliver Cromwell – world-famous, of course, for his horrible warts – then became Prime Minister and invented Parliament. He experimented with many forms of Parliament including the Long Parliament, the Short Parliament, the Rump Parliament and the Addled (or 'smelly') Parliament, before finally settling on The *Houses* of Parliament, which we still have to this day, and Big Ben, of course, the renowned clock.

The British Commonwealth

He is probably most famous, however, for inventing the British Commonwealth (or 'Empire') which is famed throughout the world and still pays homage to Her Majesty who visits it whenever she can with numerous Royal Visits, and gets a very very warm welcome whenever she does so, obviously.

So Where Was All The Cavaliers At This Time?

Meanwhile, all the Cavaliers had run off to France, where they carried on flaunting and swaggering and dolloping themselves with after-shave until the French Revolution, of course, when all the *French* Cavaliers (or *Noblesse Oblige* as they was known) started getting guillotined by all the ladies who done the knitting.

The Restoration

For this reason, they all swaggered back to England again, which was in fact, by then, the same as it had been before they'd gone, owing to the Restoration, which had come in under Charles II and Nell Dunn,[1] seeing as Oliver Cromwell had suddenly died of massive sexual repression and his son, Tony, who succeeded him as Lord Protector of All England and the Commonwealth, wasn't really suitable, being more interested in singing.

Fortunately, the Monarch and PM nowadays are no longer at war and are very good friends. They in fact know each other socially, often go on holiday together and buy each other Christmas presents, and so on. So although the Prime Minister makes the actual laws of the country, in other words makes the decisions that affect our day-to-day living – whether to have more battleships, for instance; where to have new traffic lights and so on – she will *always* check it out with the Monarch first. This happens in the famous Monday meetings at Buckingham Palace, when the PM and the entire House of Commons supplicate themselves on the floor of an ante-

---

[1] The celebrated orange-seller and mistress.

chamber and report to Her Majesty all the new Acts of Parliament that they are hoping to be making.

Obviously, if the Monarch radically objected to a particular Act, they wouldn't pass it, but this is incredibly rare because a Monarch such as ours is only too keen to help in the running of the country and knows *full well* that before an Act is presented to her by the House of Commons, Parliament has done an *enormous* amount of background research and reading about it and a lot of MPs have spent a lot of time talking about it before it all finally gets written down in old-fashioned writing on the traditional House of Commons parchment. In other words, the Monarch is hardly going to suggest chucking it all in the bin, unless she has a real and genuine reason.

In fact, Parliament and Monarchy work so closely together nowadays that it is my opinion that Parliament has been made virtually redundant and will *almost certainly be unnecessary* in a couple of years.

Parliament's Main Function

The main function of Parliament nowadays is really just to guard against the almost unthinkable event of the Queen suddenly going berserk. Obviously, the idea of our Monarch – beloved as she is across the globe, mother, grandmother, homeopath, patron of the arts – suddenly losing her rag and doing the goose-step and murdering intellectuals is unthinkable, but it is just as well to be on the safe side, as I'm sure she'd be the first to agree. Obviously this is a very delicate and sensitive area and is never actually mentioned. In other words the PM hardly goes up to the Queen and says: 'We're going to have another Parliament this year, in case you go potty.' But it is tacitly understood that that is, in fact, what Parliament is for.

Mother Of Parliament To This Day

To this day, our own House of Parliament is known as the Mother of Parliaments. This is because, following the British example, many countries had civil wars and revolutions and set up Parliaments of their own, seeing as they too had despots and tyrants they wanted to get rid of. Not that King Charles I was a despot or tyrant, obviously. No British monarch has ever been a despot, I'm happy to say. *Or* a tyrant. Charles I was, in fact, a very shy person, whose rather reclusive personality made him *appear* to be a completely unapproachable religious maniac, obsessed with himself and totally blind to the cries of his people, whereas in fact, deep down, he was a very warm-hearted person who loved nothing better than a quiet night in the bosom of his family.

There were, of course, many people at this time who *was* true despots and tyrants such as Louis XIV, Ivan the Terrible, Frederick the Great of Russia, Madame Pompidou and Mrs Beaton. These rulers obviously did certain things to benefit their people like introducing bye-laws regarding dogs and putting up fountains in parks and so forth, but they were really only interested in one thing. Going to the hairdresser and masked balls.

For this reason, there was numerous civil wars and French revolutions, in particular the French Revolution.

THINGS TO DO:

1. EITHER draw a lady and gentleman Cavalier flaunting, OR visit the Commonwealth Institute, in Kensington High Street, which still stands to this day.

2. You might also like to visit Commonwealth Way in Plumstead, Commonwealth Road in Tottenham, and Commonwealth Avenue beside London's famed Wormwood Scrubs.

CHAPTER XLV
THE AGE OF REVOLUTION

'We have all of us life to live and work to do.'

(Charlton Heston)

NOT surprisingly, Europe was now in turmoil. This was basically because most countries had copied the British Commonwealth, done their own Houses of Parliament and abolished the Monarch for good. Which is hardly the point, obviously. The whole point of Civil War is to abolish the Monarch *for a while*. Till the country gets back on its feet again. And then bring him back. Just like we done with Charles II. In other words, *don't jack the monarchy in for ever*! Otherwise all hell breaks loose, which is exactly what happened, of course, and why the whole of Europe became riven with anarchy, which is what occurs if you don't have a sensible monarch on the throne (anarchy is in fact an ancient Russian word and means precisely that: *an* = lack of; *archy* = a sensible monarch).

In fact, when you have anarchy, there are no buses, trains, schools or postmen or nothing. Everyone just does whatever he feels like doing and basically doesn't care *who* he offends in the process.

If I was an *anarchist* historian writing this book for instance, my *sole intention* would be to unnecessarily shock and offend my readers, regardless of the consequences. In other words, I might, to all intents and purposes, *appear* to be writing a perfectly normal history of the human race. But deep down within the heart of the reader – would lurk the fear that *at any moment I could simply pull out the rug from under your eyes.*

You'd be approaching the end of the page.

You'd read on as normally as you could. But all the time you'd know full well that this is the world of the anarchist where anything can happen. Where the following page might contain material of such an unnecessarily offensive nature that you might never ever again see life in the same way

As it happens it didn't.

But it could have.

And that's the point I'm making. In other words, the point about anarchy is you never know where you are with it. It *might* strike or it might not.

What I'm saying is that if *you now knew* that from any time here-on-in in this volume there could be, for example:

pages ripped out for no apparent reason;

photos of unpleasant sexual proclivities;

bits of old Swiss Roll stuck between the pages;

unnecessarily offensive remarks about leading members of the Church of England.

Then I can guarantee that your *whole emotional fabric*, as a reader of this volume, would be permanently and irrevocably impaired. *Because you would never know what was coming next* – which is precisely what the anarchist wants of course!

And why so many non-British people, like the French, for instance, are always in a state of such constant anxiety. They live their lives as best they can. But they know – deep down – that they are *play-acting at normality*. That, at any moment, Dame Anarchy and her three brothers, Shock, Outrage and Unnecessary Offence, can come bursting through the paper-thin veneer of their suburban lives.

And why is this?

Because they've all abolished their monarchs.

It is, in fact, a fascinating and strange irony that apart from Holland and Tonga, Great Britain – who was the very first country in the world to *replace* a monarch – is now the only country in the world that still *has* a monarch![1]

Unbelievable as this may seen.

---

[1] Obviously, in stating that Britain is the only country with a monarchy apart from Holland and Tonga, I am *not* forgetting Norway, Spain, Belgium, Morocco, Sweden, Denmark, Jordan, Swaziland, Saudi Arabia or Monaco, which are of course all monarchies, as my colleague has just pointed out. And for which I should once again like to thank him. What I *mean*, obviously, Wallace, is a monarchy that still takes an active and *essential* part in its country's affairs. In other words, still has Honours Lists, Royal Weddings, Changing of the Guards and Royal Tournaments and so forth. A monarchy like ours in other words. That captures the imagination of the entire world. Other countries may indeed have Royalty, but they might as well not for all we know about it! It's hardly world news, for instance, if King Gustav's sister goes on an illicit holiday to Mustique, which it certainly was when Her Royal Highness Prince Margaret did with Roddy Maude-Roxby. Or if King Leopold of the Belgians' daughter suddenly has a baby it doesn't exactly bring the world's traffic to a halt. King Leopold of Belgium hasn't got a daughter, as it happens, but she wouldn't have brought the traffic to a halt if he did have, is the point I'm making.

THINGS TO DO:

1. Make a scale model of an innocent European monarch being abolished by an anarchist.

When our own Princess of Wales, Princess Diana, on the other hand, left Queen Charlotte's Hospital with Prince William, Duke of Northumberland, in her arms, over two hundred and seventy-five thousand million people watched the evening news, which is more than four times the population of the entire world.

CHAPTER XLVI
THE AGE OF LIBERTY

'It is the nature of all greatness not to be exact.'

(Burke)

THE Age of Revolution was also known, of course, as the Age of Liberty which it's very important to have as well, obviously, and was chiefly run by the celebrated libertine Sir James Burke who, together with Sir Jack Hobbes[1] and Dennis Compton wrote some of the most famous writings against injustice, tyranny and oppression that the world has ever seen. These include *Burke's Peerage*, *Burke's Law* and *Burke and Hare – The Truth*.

THINGS TO DO:

1. Release from bondage an oppressed person of your acquaintance.

---

[1] Ancestor of the famed philosopher and kettle magnate Sir Russell Hobbes.

CHAPTER XLVII
THE INTERREGNUM

*'People will not look forward to posterity who never
look backwards to their ancestors.'*

(James Burke)

AFTER King Charles II, who died of too much sexuality with Nell
Dunn, England had a succession of Monarchs and Prime Ministers all
of whom got on very well, I'm happy to say.

The next king was William of Orange who was Nell Dunn's son of
course – hence the name. He then married Queen Mary, who begun the
tradition of the monarch giving her name to a boat, and for this reason were
called William and Mary. Then there was George I, George II, George III,
and finally George IV, who was the first British monarch not to wear a wig.

THINGS TO DO:

1. Discover the meaning of *interregnum*.

CHAPTER XLVIII

1789 – 1850 THE AGE OF TURMOIL

'His virtues were his arts.'

(James Burke)

THIS period was also known as the Age of Reason. It was a very important period and saw the birth of many new ideas that changed the face of the world in many respects and lasted till 1850.

THINGS TO DO:

1. See *Antony and Cleopatra, Soylent Green, The War Lord, The Greatest Story Ever Told, The Pigeon that took Rome* and *Planet of the Apes*, all starring Charlton Heston.

WORLD AFFAIRS: 1851

'I am about to take my last voyage. A great leap in the dark.'

(James Burke – last words)

MEANWHILE, the rest of the world more or less carried on as it had been doing and didn't really start changing yet, particularly. Such as Japan, for instance.

THINGS TO DO:

1. Précis this chapter in your own words.

CHAPTER L

THE HISTORY OF JAPAN

'So had Japan changed much in all this time?'

(Wallace)

JAPAN had basically not changed at all and was still very traditional in her customs in many respects.

Japanese People
Japanese people were ruled by Shoguns who fought numerous wars against other Shoguns, as has been demonstrated in the famous best-seller *Shogun* by James Michener and in the celebrated Japanese films, *The Magnificent Seven*, *The Magnificent Seven Rides Again* and *Seven Brides for Seven Brothers*.[1]

Japanese Customs
If they weren't fighting for a Shogun, most Japanese people's time was spent doing tea rituals, table-laquering and miniature gardening.[2]

And so it was that the mighty Japanese empire came to an end.

THINGS TO DO:

1. Make a paper model of Windsor Castle, using the traditional Japanese skill of *hari-kiri* or paper-folding.[3]

---

[1] Also *The Seventh Veil*, *The Seventh Seal*, *The Seventh Voyage of Sinbad*, *A Severed Head* and *Twelve Angry Men*.

[2] Due to Japanese overcrowding in inner cities.

[3] Japanese: *hari* = paper; *kiri* = folding.

CHAPTER LI
THE LIFE OF DOCTOR JOHNSON

'Doctor Johnson, I presume.'

(Boswell)

ONE of the most famous people to occur at this juncture was, of course, Doctor Johnson, the world-famous man of letters, although, tragically, many of his letters have been lost because the GPO was still in a very rudimentary state, without such things as automated sorting and the post code.

At the same time contemporary roads were plagued with highwaymen, so that even if a letter didn't get mislaid in a rudimentary sub-post office, it would almost certainly have got stolen *en route*. Although why a highwayman would want to steal people's letters I have no idea, seeing as most people's letters tend to be extremely dull, particularly if you don't know them.

The end of Johnson

In his later years, he gave up private practice to write the classic best-seller *Boswell's Life of Johnson*, and its sequel *Johnson's Life of Boswell* before achieving international stardom on both sides of the Atlantic as popular singer and entertainer 'Al' Johnson, whose 'Mammy, how I love you' became a 'hit' across the globe.

THINGS TO DO:

1. Describe in your own words the historic meeting between Dr Johnson and Sherlock Holmes the legendary detective, with whom he lived, of course, in London's fashionable Baker Street.

CHAPTER LII

IMPORTANT NEW DEVELOPMENTS IN THE THIRD WORLD

'I am about to take my last voyage. A great leap in the dark.'

(Doctor Johnson – last words)

IN the rest of the world, China went on being like it was, without any major new customs.

Africa of course had many customs, as it does to this day, and as did many other countries, all of whose customs was very important. Obviously customs are very important when you go into a country and when you come out of it, and have been considerably tightened up in the twentieth century, due to bomb-scares and hijackings, which is no bad thing, even if it is a bit of an inconvenience at the airport.

THINGS TO DO:

1. Using this chapter as your basis, write a detailed essay entitled: 'The Third World as I see it.'

CHAPTER LIII
THE INTERREGNUM

'Nemo benificia in calendario scribit.'
[Who benefits from a messy wall-planner?]

(Ovid)

AFTER William IV came William V or 'Rufus', then his son Edward VI, then Edward VII his son, then his son Edward VIII and finally his grandmother Queen Victoria – famed, of course, across the world and basing her world-renowned nomenclature on the legendary railway station of the same name.[1] St Pancras is probably more exotic architecturally, but her courtiers warned her against naming herself Queen Pancras for obvious medical reasons.

Queen Victoria ascended the throne at eighteen with her husband and consortium Prince Albert Hall. Together with some of the greatest Prime Ministers known to man, her mighty legs bestraddled the peeping world like a Colossus, bringing light to the starving and bread to them as grieved without redress. And the names of those men, her Prime Ministers, will be remembered too and honoured for all time. Men who dedicated their whole lives and sacrificed all, often working late into the night, to bring a ray of hope to their despairing fellows. Men like Robert Walpole, Pitt the Elder, Pitt the Younger, Disraeli, Neville Chamberlain, The Old Pretender, The Blue Boy, Charles de Gaulle, Lord Reith, Scott of the Antarctic, Fagin, Kenneth Robinson, Charles Pratt the First Earl of Camden, Dirk Bogarde and Robinson Crusoe.

[1] Victoria Station.

THE INTERREGNUM

THINGS TO DO:

1. Describe in not more than five thousand words each the reasons behind the following:

a. The War of Austrian Succession.

b. The Corn Laws.

c. The Black Hole of Calcutta.

d. Charles Pratt, the first Earl of Camden.

CHAPTER LIV

THE NAPOLEONIC WARS

'Friendship is a golden chain,
The links are friends so dear
And like a rare and precious jewel
It's treasured more each year.'

(Helen Steiner Rice – *Just for You*)

THE Napoleonic Wars

These were fought at approximately this time and were begun by Napoleon, as the name implies.

The End of the Napoleonic Wars

Meanwhile, the end of the Napoleonic Wars occurred at the Battle of Trafalgar Square which was won, of course, by the Admiral Lord Nelson who was famous for losing an eye and an arm and being killed at the same time.

The Results of the Napoleonic Wars

As a result of the Napoleonic Wars, Napoleon was exiled to Cuba, where he was also born, of course, during his early childhood, and where he now returned to live with his ageing grandparents. They tried to interest him in draughts, orienteering and home wine-brewing but such pursuits held little joy for one for who had wielded such power as he had done.

Meanwhile, his parents, wife and children had all moved into the Palace of Versailles and refused to have anything to do with him, while his father Denis Napoleon, a plumber, set himself up as Napoleon II. Immediately, Napoleon – now Napoleon I, obviously – escaped, disguised as a washerwoman, and arrived in Paris a week later ready to proclaim himself once again Emperor of all the Frances.

In the meantime, however, and unbeknown to him, his father Napoleon II had been deposed by his nephew, seventeen-year-old Maxim Napoleon who was then deposed by distant Auntie Elaine Napoleon who became Napoleon IV and had just started on the Arc de Triomphe when she was deposed by Napoleon V, a total stranger from Nîmes, who happened to have the same name.

She then re-deposed Napoleon V and became Napoleon VI but then got deposed herself by Napoleon's father, Denis, who had been Napoleon II and now became Napoleon VII. He was then deposed by Maxim, who a few weeks later got deposed by his own mother, who in turn got deposed by Napoleon's grandfather who'd come over from Cuba to try his hand, but lasted only a couple of weeks before two gentlemen from Australia deposed him, who *called* themselves Napoleon, although nobody ever found out whether they in fact were or not.

For this reason, when the original Napoleon arrived in Paris a week later in his home-made hang-glider, and applied to the government to be Emperor again, he had to settle for being Napoleon XIII. Disappointed but unperturbed, he crowned himself in the Louvre and exhorted the people of France to rally around him. Obviously the people of France had already rallied round the twelve other Napoleons, so there were very few French people left to rally round anyone. In fact, all he could find was a couple of gardeners in the Bois de Boulogne and a few elderly porters at the Gare d'Austerlitz, most of whom thought he was Louis XIV anyway.

Napoleon

Together they met at the famous Battle of Waterloo in South London. But Napoleon's old powers were waning. He had lost a lot of hair, besides which his right hand had mysteriously vanished. For this reason, the battle was won by the Duke of Wellington, the legendary Duke.

Over the next thirty years, Napoleon made various attempts to set himself up as Napoleon XVII, XXIII, XXIX, XXXI, XLV, LIV, LXIII and LXXVI, but the days of his greatness was over and he became a mere shadow of his former self, rapidly declining into embittered senility in his Cuban twilight home.

For Sidney Wellington, of course, it was a whole different kettle of fish. He returned to a hero's welcome and, in his honour, both Waterloo Station *and* Underground were built. He had in fact asked for a statue like

Nelson on top of a two-hundred-foot plinth facing the Mall and Bucking-ham Palace, but the Arts Council who financed war memorials, as they still do of course, had nothing left in its non-regional budget, so he had to settle for Waterloo, which isn't bad, considering it serves nearly the whole of the south of England. Trains running, obviously.

THINGS TO DO:

1. Paint a famous portrait of Horatio Nelson mortally wounded on the bridge of his flagship the Cutty Sark, surrounded by his best friend, Thomas Hardy, author of *Bead the Obscure*, *Tess* and *Out of Africa*.

2. Decide which of the following is the most likely place for Napoleon to have lost his hand:

a. The Eiffel Tower.
b. Crossing the Channel.
c. Waterloo Station.
d. In the guillotine.

LITTLE-KNOWN THEORIES NO. 1

There is a rather intriguing theory that is currently gaining some credence in historical circles and is my own theory, as it happens, namely that Nelson and Napoleon were in fact *one and the same person*, owing to the similarity in names and hats and the fact that they only had the one hand. The only hole in this theory is how one man could have been both Nelson and Napoleon in the Battle of Trafalgar Square without anyone else knowing, i.e. how he could have got from one flagship to the other, changed costumes, had himself killed as Nelson, nipped back to being Napoleon again, then back to being Nelson to have himself buried at sea and *then* back in time for Napoleon's victory celebrations in Paris? Unfortunately, there is no easy answer to this fascinating historical riddle. Suffice it to say, in the immortal last words of Sir Thomas Hardy: 'There's more to this than meets the eye, in my opinion.'

CHAPTER LV

THE AMERICAN WAR OF INDEPENDENCE

'Yanky doodle, keep it up
Yanky doodle dandy.'

(American National Anthem)

AMERICA, of course was still being run by the British Government at this time so a number of people decided to start the famous American War of Independence. Now I think it's very important to make it *absolutely clear* at this juncture that this had nothing to do with anything the British was doing wrong, obviously. In other words, there wasn't a load of British nobles keeping the Americans as serfs or in bondage or anything of that ilk.

I'm sure that American historians would be the first to admit that the British Government ruled America very very well indeed, but that the Americans just thought: 'Well, we've been here 200 years now. We have our own accents, our own recipes, our own hobbies. Surely we can govern our own country.'

So they sent off to George III and said: 'Could we run America now?' Now, I am quite certain that, under normal circumstances, George III would have been only too delighted to accede to this request but, unfortunately, he had, at this time, a rather intimate ailment which affects first the 'personal' areas, if you get my meaning, and then the brain, so that he was now talking to trees and sleeping with his horse, so he said: 'No, absolutely out of the question' and sent the entire British army – the famed 'Red Coats' – to the US under Lord Butcher Cumberland; the well-known unpopular general. They had numerous battles, particularly the Boston Tea-Party, The Gettysburg Address and the Battle of the Bulge, but the Confederates or Yankee Doodles, as they was known, being more conversant with the terrain and not having the red coats obviously, won.

For this reason, America became independent and had the Declaration of Independence under George Washington which meant they were now American and not British, but would obviously always respect and admire Britain a great deal and always remember to give thanks to Britain for her many years of wise and beneficial Government, and would therefore have a special day each year to mark their gratitude which would be called 'Thanksgiving Day', in other words a special day to thank Britain for all its help in getting America off the ground, so to speak, which is, in fact, their equivalent of our Christmas Day, when everybody has turkey and presents and crackers and so forth.

For this reason, and it's hardly surprising when you think about it, the Americans decided to run the country on very British lines, which they do to this day except they don't have a Monarch but a President, who lives more like a Monarch *than* a Monarch, if you ask me, judging by the size of the White House and the astronomic number of rooms in it, which, after all, only have to accommodate Mr and Mrs Reagan, Mr and Mrs Bush, Henry Kissinger and a few aides. Unlike our own PM who lives very humbly indeed in Number 10 Downing Street with a massive staff in only two bedrooms.

THINGS TO DO:

1. Make a scale model of the Battle of the Bulge.

CHAPTER LVI

THE NINETEENTH CENTURY

'But facts are chiels that winna ding.'

(Burns)

THE nineteenth century occurred straight after the American War of Independence and is chiefly remembered for European turmoil, Lord Macaulay and The Industrial Revolution which suddenly broke out at this time.

Reasons Behind the Industrial Revolution

The reasons behind the Industrial Revolution was mainly all the numerous inventions that started being made by various inventors at this time, such as Crompton's Mule by James Arkwright;[1] Stevenson's Rocket by James Herriot; Wordsworth's Prelude by Robert Louis Stevenson; and the Electric Kettle by Watt Tyler. Not to mention Constable's Haywain, Thompson's Gazelle, the Reader's Digest and Scott's Porage Oats. All of which were discovered during this momentous age. Needless to say, however, it wasn't all a patch of bluebells.

Before the Industrial Revolution

Before the Industrial Revolution, virtually the whole country lived in the country, generally in Dorset, and spent their lives clog-dancing, sheep-dipping, making haystacks, and selling home-made doylies.[2]

[1] Also Arkwright's Mule, of course, by Crompton.

[2] From the French *de oylé*: *de* = for prevention of; *oylé* = unsightly grease. Doylies were introduced in rural communities to prevent butter dripping off muffins on to the furniture, which, of course, was all antique and therefore costly to clean.

143

The Industrial Revolution

Suddenly, however, the Industrial Revolution occurred and within days factories and coalmines started going up all over Europe. Immediately tiny cuddly ponies were shipped down from the Shetlands to drag massively heavy iron barges full of granite rocks the entire length of the Manchester Ship Canal while pathetically starving babies of four or five weeks with scurvy and malaria were forced up chimneys the second they were out of nappies or dragooned into hauling huge railway trucks laden with massive ton weights of coal uphill for miles through pitch-black airless rat-infested winding tunnels prone to collapse at any minute. A tradition still carried on in many Yorkshire pits to this day.

The Industrial Revolution is also responsible of course for many very famous shops. These include Etam, Dorothy Perkins, Waitrose, Londis, W. H. Smith and Boots. Although the most famous in my opinion is, without any shadow of a doubt, Marks and Spencers which is run, of course, by the famous art-loving Earl, Lord Sheath, or Spencer as he likes to be known, for obvious reasons.

Yoghurt, cottage cheese and prawn-flavoured petals[1] all emanated from his fascinating and teeming brain. Although probably his greatest invention was male underpants which have revolutionized men's private areas the world over.

THINGS TO DO:

1. Construct this simple 1892 *Parsons Radial Flow Steam Turbine Engine* (*see illus. opposite*) – the first steam turbine to surpass in efficiency a reciprocated engine of equal output.

---

[1] And a favourite – may I add – of my own mother Mrs Dingle (*see* Chapter LVIII – 'The Twentieth Century'.)

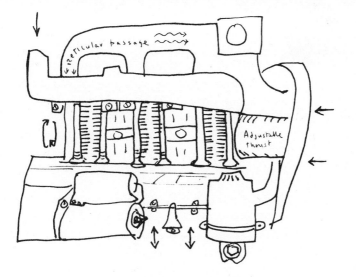

1892 The Parsons Radial Flow Steam Turbine Engine.

Instructions for use:
The steam enters through a double governor valve and then flows radially from the centre to the circumference of six wheels, arranged in series with concentric rows of blading, alternating with fixed rows on the diaphragms. The steam then passes from one to the next by reticular passages formed in the diaphragms. The longitudinal pressure exerted on the turbine shafts is counterbalanced by a grooved piston at the HP end of the shaft, excess pressure being taken by the adjustable thrust block which locates the rotor.
Don't forget the flexible coupling to the alternator shaft.

CHAPTER LVII

THE VOTE

'Hoc erat in votis. Modus agri non ita magnus.
Hortus ubi et tecto vicinus jugis aquae fons
Et paulum silvae super his foret. Auctius atque
Di melius fecere. Bene est.'
(It's very important everyone has the vote in my opinion)

(Horace)[1]

ANYWAY, as soon as word reached Queen Victoria and the Government's ears about all the babies and ponies being shoved up chimneys, they immediately commenced doing numerous reforms, particularly in regarding the Vote, which is a crucial feature of a democracy such as ours and without which society would collapse instantaneously.

Up until this time, of course, only the nobility had the vote, which means that out of a population of three hundred and twenty-nine million there was a total electorate of fifty-three so that election results tended to be a somewhat foregone conclusion.

On Polling Day, the nobles would arrive in their carriages, have a glass of champagne with the candidate, put their cross on the card, have another glass of champagne with the candidate and gallop off to a point-to-point in Shipton-under-Wychwood. Minutes later, the result would be announced by a tiny black boy in blue satin with a white wig.

Here is a result typical of the time:-

Con	52	Ind	0
Lab	0	Ecol	0
Lib/SDP	1		

---

[1] The famous Greek poet. Surname unknown.

146

This obviously was not overly popular with the rest of the population who, for this reason, had the famous Jarrow March. And people even poorer than themselves came out of their houses and gave them mugs of tea, boots, biscuits and packets of Trex as they camped beside The Great North Road and the nobles' carriages splashed by and they sang together, songs of the dignity of man, beneath the slow-turning starry sky.

And so it was they met the Queen. On a cold and wintry Christmas Eve. And she rode out alone on her horse, Black Beauty, to meet them on Wimbledon Common and a huge hush went over the massive crowd and she spoke gently to their leaders, Jack Cade and Dorothy Perkins, and assured them that everyone would have the vote from hereon in; and that all factories would be pulled down; and no one would catch bronchitis down the mines no more; and that everything would be made by robots; and everyone would have an equal share of the gigantic profit; and live in little thatched cottages and be totally self-sufficient and swop vegetables and play the flute and write poems and children would roam and skip in the sun-dappled forests and green-carpeted English hills and have no disease for evermore.

This was obviously not actually possible, owing to the fact that the British Government had already spent millions of pounds on various crucial things like the Indian Mutiny, the Zulu Wars, Khartoum and the Ideal Home Exhibition, and had also borrowed quite a few more million pounds from the International Monetary Fund or IBA, as it is known – a massive building society in Switzerland. But, obviously, Queen Victoria couldn't be expected to know all that, seeing as money is a very very complicated business, as any financial expert will tell you. Particularly for a busy monarch.

All the same, she spoke to the marchers gently and with understanding and courteously answered their queries. Then, after she had gone home to a roaring fire and family Christmas at Balmoral, they were beaten up by mounted police with long staves who charged them down where they stood so they wouldn't do it again.

And they lay shivering all night on the frozen ground and most of them died. Including little children. Then they went home to Jarrow.

The Enfranchisement of the Franchise
And all the factories carried on churning out identical tumblers and grey lino until the great Australian Prime Minister, Lord Melbourne, saw how depressing all the products were and persuaded the Government to let everyone have a vote finally, which meant that everyone could vote for who they wanted which meant that not surprisingly the Conservatives took a bit of a tumble, particularly seeing as their election platform was the abolition of admission charges to gymkhanas and the injection of all workers with compulsory rickets.

As a result the Whig Party swept to power on the platform of free wigs for all, although this was hardly surprising, seeing as the cost of wigs at the time was extortionate and failure to wear an adequate wig, toupee or hairpiece punishable by hanging.[1] The Conservatives retaliated, therefore, by offering everyone free dinners and their own time-share villa on the Costa del Sol. So the Whigs changed their name to Labour and offered to blow the Conservatives up and give everyone a free car, so the Conservatives changed their name to Tories and offered the entire population £500,000 each and the abolition of all Income Tax (including arrears). Then Prince Albert died, and Queen Victoria – who was just about to step in and put an end to all this vote-catching nonsense – went delirious and abolished sex. Which went on for the next seventy years until she died in 1938.

The Emaciation of Women
This period was also very important for emaciating women. Many of whom were outraged at the fact that only men got the vote and they weren't allowed to, which is absurd, obviously, seeing as women are human beings the same as everyone else. The leader of the women in their struggle for emaciation was the famous majorette, Mrs Pankhurst, who chained herself to Buckingham Palace and committed numerous other atrocities on herself to bring the plight of women to the attention of the Queen, who was a woman, after all, but who had unfortunately gone berserk, owing to Albert having died, and ordered Mrs Pankhurst lashed to two sets of frenzied stallions galloping in opposite directions.

Fortunately this particular form of punishment had been repealed by Alfred the Great so she was given a life sentence in Dartmoor, suspended for six thousand years. Undeterred, women led marches, held conferences, wore trousers, had women-only dances, became bus conductors and sat in circles with the moon painted on their brows. All of which had a profound effect on men who started breaking down in the street, going into psychoanalysis and weeping openly for no apparent reason.

This is known as the birth of feminism. And, speaking as a feminist – seeing as I am regarded as a feminist by many very feminist women – I would like to say that I believe that women still deserve full emaciation and I – along with many women – will not rest until this day has been achieved.

Obviously, having said this, I think it is very important to make clear that while I am an extremely *feminist* person, it goes without saying obviously that I am not in any way a *feminine* person. In other words, what

---

[1] The price of wigs has fortunately declined dramatically in recent years and for this reason they are now enjoying a colossal return to popularity. A recent survey in fact showed that over ninety per cent of the population of the world now wears a wig. Here are a number of world-famous wig wearers: President Mubarak of Egypt, Andrea Papandreou of Greece, Queen Juliana of the Netherlands and, of course, our own Neil Kinnock.

I'm saying is that it is perfectly possible for the more rugged and masculine type of man, such as myself, to be deeply sympathetic to the Feminist Cause without losing any of the quintessential maleness of his fundamental masculinity. As many young ladies would certainly testify with regard to myself, as it happens! Although not in *too* much detail, hopefully, particularly about what goes on in my penthouse after a bottle of Veuve Clicquot and a couple of flambéd steaks with the lights down low and Richard Clayderman[1] whispering from the walls, if you get my meaning.

Exploration

At the same time, many British people were discovering large areas of the known world, such as Dr Livingstone, who discovered Africa and Stanley, who discovered Dr Livingstone.

The Historic Meeting of Stanley and Livingstone. One of the most legendary meetings of all time.

Meanwhile Australia and the South Pacific were discovered by Thomas Cook and Son, the North Pole by Sir Timothy Leary and Saudi Arabia by Sir Richard Burton who, disguised as an Arab oil-lamp expert, managed to penetrate into Mecca itself, the famed Islamic dance hall. Sir Richard returned home, of course, to become one of the greatest actors of this century and made some of the finest films ever made including *Exorcist II*, *Equus*, *Alexander the Great*, *Cleopatra* and *Where Eagles Dare*.

---

[1] The internationally renowned classical pianist.

Numerous Crucial Wars

During the Victorian era, the British led the world in numerous crucial wars against numerous other parts of the world who was laying their hands on numerous other parts of the world. These were:

1. *The Crimean War,* in which the Russians was laying their cruel hand on the Crimeans and was therefore known as 'the Eastern Question', which the British cleared up pretty swiftly, of course, under Florence Nightingale.

2. *The Zulu War, The Indian Mutiny* and *Khartoum,* in which the Zulus, Indians and Sudanese were in fact laying their hands on Zululand, India and the Sudan, which is fair enough, in a manner of speaking, seeing as they was, one could generally argue, the people who lived there. Unfortunately, however, we must now leave these fascinating and complex events, seeing as clearly it is not possible in a volume of this world-embracing length to deal adequately with the numerous whys and wherefores of all the intricate, sensitive and delicate issues involved. The story of Khartoum was, of course, the subject of the famous film *Khartoum,* directed by snooker wizard Sir Basil Reardon and starring for the first time *together on the same screen* both Charlton Heston as General Gordon Richards *and* Sir Laurence Olivier as the infamous Sudanese madman, the Mardy. Charlton Heston, of course, also played General Richards in that other famous war:

3. *55 Days at Peking,* chronicling the infamous Boxing Day rebellion in which thousands of martial arts and kung fu fanatics under the deranged Empress Madam Ming The Merciless, played by ballet star Sir Robert Helpman, attempted to murder a number of defenceless lady missionaries and little Chinese children, all of whom were rescued by the British Government and taken home to help in the Industrial Revolution.

Chinese Rice Salesman

THE VOTE

THINGS TO DO:

1. Write a nineteenth-century novel.

2. Visit the following famous nineteenth-century landmarks: Westminster Abbey, Tower Bridge, Piccadilly Circus, Shipton-under-Wychwood, the Arts Council of Great Britain, Khartoum.

3. Read *The Secret Diary of Sir Peter Hall* by Sir Peter Hall. (Pub. Hamish Hamilton. Price £5.95, UK only.) And worth every penny if I may say so. A book that changed my life. I'm sure it will change yours.

CHAPTER LVIII

THE TWENTIETH CENTURY

'Everything is becoming Hamlet.'

(Sir Peter Hall – *The Secret Diary of Peter Hall*)

MEANWHILE, Europe was in turmoil. In Russia, Czar Nicholas I came under the sinister influence of the horribly bearded Rasputin. Portrayed, of course, by Tom Baker in the famous film *Fanny and Alexander* and loved by kiddies across the globe as Dr Who, Rasputin inveigled Nicholas and his wife Anastasia into spending the entire Russian budget on an ever-increasing round of 'adult' parties and threesomes in Leningrad. For this reason, the Russian peasants, who had lived on a diet of their own shoes, snow and disused balalaika strings for the last nine hundred years, decided to hold the Russian Revolution, which is hardly surprising. Thus it was that Karl Marx, who was also bearded, and Vladimir Lennon, who was less bearded but bald, led the seventy-five million barefoot peasants up the Odessa steps and over the shattered chandeliers of the Moscow Winter Gardens to do unspeakable things to Rasputin and start Communism, which many Russian people still are to this day obviously.

Rasputin – the famed maniac

The First World War

Meanwhile, in Germany, Kaiser Wilhelm 'Bill' II and the Bismarck started the First World War which they lost, fortunately.

The Roaring Twenties

After which was the Roaring Twenties, famous for the Charleston,[1] and the Thirties, which were very depressing.

The Second World War

These were then followed by the Second World War which was started by the Germans once *again*, I'm sorry to say, and won, of course, by the English.

1945

1945 was probably the most crucial year in the history of the Earth, besides which it was also a crucial year in my own life, as it happens. This is because it was – staggeringly – *the year I was born.*

I say 'staggeringly' because people are always staggered when they hear this, having usually made the assumption from my photographs (*see* the jacket of this volume, for instance) and my theatrical and televisual appearances that I am considerably younger. Usually in my mid- to late twenties.

However – remarkable as it may seem – I was truly born in 1945.

In fact, and not many people know this, I actually made my 'first appearance' as it were to the actual sounds of the Bells of Victory themselves. As the first great cry of 'Freedom' echoed across the nations. (And, infant though I was, how will I forget that sound?).

For, believe it or not, *I was born at the stroke of midnight on the very last day of World War II.* My mother – Mrs Evadne Dingle – going into labour actually *during* those last darkest hours. As the peace of the world teetered in the balance and she strode on through the Blitz with her tea and biscuits – helping the needy, encouraging the destitute, defusing unexploded bombs, even collecting wet dish-cloths for the great nightly effort to douse St Paul's, before finally hearkening to the pleas of those thousands of East-enders, whom she was at that moment personally helping to drag from the rubble of their homes, begging her to look to herself and her as yet unborn foetus.

And so – the Battle of Britain raging all about her – she finally reached Piccadilly Tube air-raid shelter, in the heart of London's East End. And there it was that I was born, a breech delivery as it happens,[2] in the cramped

---

[1] A rather interesting amalgam of the names Charlton and Heston which as yet appears to have been noticed only by myself.

[2] And one of the most difficult and most dangerous births there is, of course. Particularly in the Underground.

privacy of a London Transport junction box, because there was no room for her on the platform. And still it moves me as I think of her, bearing my little unborn self through those last desperate months of wartime with only one boiled potato, three Brussel sprouts and a tea-spoon of skimmed milk to sustain her and yet thinking never of herself but only of others in their need.

Little did she know, of course, that to have spared her some of her ante-natal discomfort and to have had the chance, however brief, to assist in the War Effort myself, I would willingly have been born many months premature. As it happens, I was born three months late, her labour lasted sixteen weeks and I weighed four and a half stone at birth. Something I have never forgiven myself for. And just one of the many personal burdens I still carry to this day. Why was it, I find myself wondering, *that I resisted my own birth for so long?*

This is, of course, an example of what is known to psychoanalysts and neurosurgeons as *birth traumas* which are very upsetting, obviously, as anyone recently born will tell you, and will often affect us and dominate us for the rest of our lives *without us knowing it*, and cause no end of problems.

Birth Traumas

To this end, I have recently begun looking very deeply into my own personal *birth traumas* that I had when I was born and, for this reason, I have begun a special breathing process in which you lie in a sleeping bag in a flat with thirty other people and breathe in and out without stopping for three hours solid. Besides looking at your *birth traumas*, this method also enables you to acquire ancient psychic powers and release the hidden Forces of the Universe and thus achieve the fulfilment of your every dream, such as massive wealth. While you do the breathing, a lady in a kimono called Janet Sunshine lights candles and strokes your brows and various other parts (though none of *my* other parts, I'm glad to say, not that I'd have been overly perturbed if she had, obviously, seeing as I am no stranger to the female touch, as is well known of course, and anyway I had my suit on) and whispers in your ear that you are incredibly perfect and beautiful. I assumed that she was whispering this to myself and a few selected participants, but soon realized she was in fact whispering the same thing to everyone, which was a surprise, to say the least, seeing as, though I agreed in some cases, and they agreed in mine presumably, it has to be said that not *all* the people there could in all honesty be described as 'beautiful', or even particularly attractive. In fact some of them were unbelievably ugly. Still, *chacun à son goût* which I suppose is the point.

As it happens, I never actually succeeded in facing all my *birth traumas* or releasing my hidden Forces seeing as, regrettably, I misunderstood the breathing instructions a little bit and in fact attempted to breathe out *without* breathing in first. This I managed to keep up for approximately five and a half minutes before I finally collapsed and, in fact, died. For this reason I am in fact *the first person ever* to have actually died during a Life Affirming Breath Workshop.

The Second World War

Nevertheless, as painful as it was to be born during the Second World War, I am now confident that my experience of those defiant years – even though they were over before I was in fact born – gave me a strength and resilience, an ability to remain level-headed throughout all adversity and a profound inner humility that are now the hallmarks of my personality and without which, I am convinced, I would never be standing where I am today. To be an impresario, historian, scientist, playwright, doctor, expert in the para-normal, actor, therapist, conjuror and osteopath at the age of forty-two is no mean feat, even though I say it myself.[1]

[1] In other words, there can't be many up-and-coming young writers of my age who have been personally commissioned, out of the blue as it were, by Sir Geoffrey Methuen himself who is not only Mogul of the most important publishing house in the world (and recognized by authors as considerably more prestigious than all other publishers at this time, such as Penguin's, Chatto and Windus, Secker and Warburg and Patricia Routledge and Kegan Paul) but has also become a very close personal friend and is also a confidant of royalty and numerous other famous people. I mention this not to blow my own trumpet, obviously, but to dispel the Dickensian Myth that publishers are stuffy old fools who can only see to the end of their last book cover. Sir Geoffrey is not a well man, as I have mentioned. He is in his nineties and is often racked with advanced senility (no joke if you're in the publishing business, as any publisher will tell you). Nevertheless, like all true pioneers, he chanced his arm on me, recognizing that it is only through backing new literary blood, such as mine, that the current stranglehold of mediocrity into which the British writing scene is currently plunged can finally be broken. I am obviously not referring to *all* new British writers here. Like John Fowles, for instance, or M. M. Kaye who wrote *The Far Pavilions* but I think it would be fair to say that it is a generally well-known fact that British writing is currently going through the severest doldrums the world has ever known, as I'm sure Mr Kaye would be the first to admit.

THINGS TO DO:

1. Describe in your own words any *birth traumas* you have recently had.

2. Visit London's famous Cabinet War Rooms where Winston Churchill and the Cabinet and their families all lived during the war. They have been left of course exactly as they were and still stand in the cellar of No. 10 Downing Street, making a truly fascinating day out for the whole family (open Tuesday to Sunday: 10–5; and on Easter Monday and all Bank Holidays. Closed Mondays; New Year's Day; Good Friday; Christmas and Boxing Day). If you're lucky you might just catch a glimpse of the Cabinet, busy arguing over a new Act. Or even spot the PM *herself* hurrying upstairs to a top-level meeting or taking a well-earned nap in the back garden.

CHAPTER LIX
THE FIFTIES

'And thence came the fifties.' (Anon)

THEN after the War came the fifties when everything was rebuilt, such as the slums.

The fifties was also famous for the Coronation, the ascent of Everest, the discovery of ITV, Wimbledon, cars and the construction of the Suez Canal by Cecil Rhodes. This vastly reduced the length of boat trips to Australia but came as a deep shock to the Egyptians who had no idea he was doing it. It therefore became known as the Suez Crisis and severely rocked the Tory Government who for this reason introduced prescription charges and inflation.

THINGS TO DO:

1. Construct your own *Mystic Egyptian Pyramid*, based on authentic plans and writings of the Ancient Pharaohs that have recently come into my possession and which I am now able to reveal to the modern world. The Pyramids, as we discovered in Chapter XIV, were not roofs, as was originally thought, but tombs. However, it was by lying inside them *before* they died that the ancient Egyptians managed not only to amass colossal wealth and immunity from illness but also, in many cases, actually attained immortal life. And are, therefore, STILL ALIVE TO THIS DAY.[1]

---

[1] It is my belief, for instance, that Omar Sharif is in fact an ancient Egyptian Pharaoh who has attained immortal life via the use of the Mystic Pyramid method. He probably has his own full-size pyramid in his Cairo apartment but keeps a portable handy for when he's filming.

Instructions for use:

The Initiate should lie naked but for a white shroud on a slab of granite in the very centre of the pyramid and simply will unto him all that which he so desireth. For those who do not wish a full-sized Mystic Pyramid (height: 481 feet; base area: 12½ acres), it is of course possible to construct a miniature pyramid to wear on the head (*see* plate 5) and more convenient for Board Meetings, travelling, jogging etc.

I would like to say that I have personally used the Mystic Pyramid and can unequivocally state that it is responsible for much of my own massive success.

CHAPTER LX
THE SIXTIES

'My head was so full of Saturday with things I had to do this weekend that I had a very bad night, and was up before four today working away until half past seven, when I went back to bed for an hour and a half.'

(Sir Peter Hall – *The Secret Diary of Peter Hall*)

THE sixties was famous for youth, chiefly, who became particularly numerous at this time. This was mainly as a result of the world-famous popular singing duo, The Beatles, who was prodigiously successful and done numerous hit records, for instance, 'I Can't Get no Satisfaction' and 'Hound Dog'. For this reason, they became household names and modern youth rebelled against their parents causing havoc across the world. Besides many things, the Beatles also started hippies who became the latest craze for many years, and contraceptives.

The Space Race
Also in the sixties, the space race began and the Russians put the first living creature in space, the famous Russian dog pilot Lenin who, although she successfully piloted a Sputnik round the moon for seven and a half months, returned home appallingly thin and neurotic, seeing as, before her, no-one realized that space has no gravity so she spent the entire journey floating upside down and unable to reach the tubes containing her dinner and pudding (*see* artist's lifelike reconstruction – not suitable for juvenile viewing).

On subsequent journeys, doggie cosmonauts Samovar, Chekhov and Zhivago were given special suction footpads and a unique automatic 'walkies' belt that operated continually through the flight, only stopping for food and sleep at four-hour intervals. The only tragedy occurred during

A. The Tragedy of 'Lenin' (artist's reconstruction)

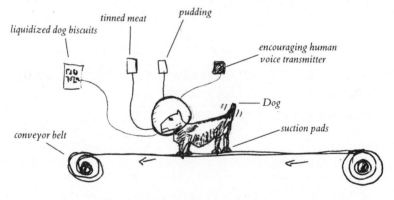

B. The Flight of Samovar

C. The Profumo Affair

the flight of Zhivago – when the automatic pilot, PAL 2000, went berserk, turned off the central heating and force-fed her for four hours at a time without any walkies. She splashed down in the Black Sea totally unslept, tragically obese and frozen to her basket.

The Profumo Affair
Refers to the famous affair between Christine Keeler and the well-known MP Giacomo Profumo who, being Italian, tended to be somewhat volatile when it came to his proclivities. Unfortunately, this story has been much sensationalized so I have no wish to go into it in any further detail.

Save to say that it also involved Mandy Rice-Davies and a bevy of scantily-clad seventeen-year-old nymphettes getting up to a considerable amount of hanky-panky with a number of costumed celebrities including most of the Tory Party, the House of Lords, the BBC and the Russians.

Once again this severely rocked the Tory Government who therefore doubled prescription charges, joined the Common Market and introduced VAT.

THINGS TO DO:

1. Read *Lady Chatterley's Lover* written in the sixties by famous pornographic miner, D. H. Lawrence.

2. Make a scale model of Twiggy.

CHAPTER LXI
THE SEVENTIES

'Do not despair, that you cannot change
The world in a day or two.
Instead, just give your very best
In the little things you do.'

(Thomas C. Gallagher)

THE seventies was chiefly famous for Watergate and numerous techno-
logical advances such as Concorde and music centres.

THINGS TO DO:

1. Write short notes on the following:
   a. Concorde
   b. music centres
   c. Watergate
   d. the seventies

CHAPTER LXII
THE EIGHTIES

'Look before you leap.'

(Mao Tse-Tung)

THE eighties – the mighty epoch during which we are currently occurring – is famous, of course, for the Mary Rose, in-car telephones, the Royal Wedding of Prince Charles to the Princess of Wales and urban decay.

THINGS TO DO:

1. Write an essay entitled: 'What I would do with the world if it was up to me, given the stage it's at.'

CHAPTER LXIII
THE COLD WAR

'The ways deep, the days short, the sun farthest off,
the very dead of winter.'

(Bishop Lancelot Andrewes)

ALTHOUGH there is no World War at this time, Russia and America now have a Cold War instead, which means they both have the Bomb which they threaten to drop on each other during disagreements.

Obviously if they did drop the Bomb on each other the world would be a nuclear winter and for this reason everyone now lives in a permanent state of anxiety seeing as it could go off at any time but no one knows when. In other words, all it takes is for someone to trip on a bit of carpet in the Kremlin or go potty for a couple of seconds in the Oval Office and wallop. In other words, the human race could all just die at any moment basically. This has greatly increased things like blood pressure and fear and so forth.

THINGS TO DO:

1. Sod all.

CHAPTER LXIV

THE END OF THE WORLD

'And the whole world will end like nobody's business.'

(*The Baghdadvita*)

I CAN now report that scientists have recently discovered a buried monastery high in the Himalayas in which were found a number of ancient forbidden parchments containing prophecies of the future of mankind done by a select band of ancient llamas.

I have been fortunate enough to obtain authentic translations of these forbidden parchments and can now report that we are, in fact, slap in the middle of the Age of Destruction, Darkness, Fire and War, otherwise known as *Kali Yuga* (Indian: *Kali* = Age of; *Yuga* = Destruction, Darkness, Fire and War), and that everything will end at about this time, with all the leaders of the earth despoiling their subjects and chucking bombs throughout the world and the stars falling from the sky like untimely figs everywhere and the sun becoming black as sackcloth of hair and all the mountains moving from where they had stood previous and heaven departing like a scroll rolling up.

THINGS TO DO:

1. Paint an ancient llama.

CHAPTER LXV
THE FUTURE

'Then there was silence in heaven for half an hour.'

(*The Bible*)

BUT let us not end this mighty Work – hand-drawn like jewels from the storm-racked ocean bed of my soul and penned into the early hours of many mornings – on a despairing note.

For while it is incontrovertibly true that a number of very high-up ancient Eastern mystics have prophesied that the Twentieth Century will be the Age of Destruction, Darkness, Fire and War and everything will end and fall away at about this time, I have also been fortunate enough to obtain authentic translations of *further* forbidden parchments, done by numerous Eskimo and Indian Shamans, as it happens, that categorically state that after the darkness, fire and war and so forth there will be a time of light when a mighty still voice will speak and open the door on the silence of everyone's stillmost core, and peace will fall on everyone like the radiant light of the morning. Which is a bit of luck, obviously.

In fact, it was shortly after reading about the Shamans, who are holy men who go on long pilgrimages into the wilderness during which they befriend wild things, converse with the spirits of the earth and plants and so forth and have visions concerning the future of the whole world, that I had a dream, as I lay tossing and turning on my unslept-on bed, wrestling with numerous problems of a financial and personal nature. And in the dream I was taken to a field in the dead of night and the clouds parted and I saw all the stars and planets in the universe before me and there was a noise such as I'd never heard before and a massive UFO landed all covered in lights in the middle of the field and the doors opened and I was invited inside and taken up many miles above the earth and shown everything.

And an extra-terrestrial guide appeared with a big head and little arms and a light that come from the pores of his skin and said to me:

'Desmond Olivier Dingle, we are the Sentinels of the Universe and you are now a prophetic shaman. There is only you and a few others what we speak to. For you are the Chosen Ones and hast all been chosen for a mighty task.'
'For what task hast we been chosen?' I asked, slipping easily into extra-terrestrial parlance.
'To lead all earthly beings out of the darkness into which it is currently sinking.'
'Anything else?'
'Not at this juncture.'
'But how will I do this, Sentinel?' I asked, with trepidation, yet with no fear did I feel.
'The exact means whereby you will enlighten the world will be revealed to you by other more high-up sentinels.'

And so I awoke and immediately felt a great and inexplicable joy, a joy so powerful that I could not restrain it but had to burst immediately into song, right where I lay on my unslept-on bed.

Whether what I dreamt was a dream or really happened, I know not, but I now believe that I have had a very profound inner knowledge revealed to me on a deeply subliminal plane. In fact on probably the *most deeply subliminal plane it's possible to reach without being dead first.* In other words, it is my humble belief that I, Desmond Olivier Dingle, have now become an extra-terrestrial shamanic prophet.
Of whom there are only about six on the entire planet probably.
Scattered about on different continents.

So do I look any different as a result?
Well, to the ordinary person in the street, I am no different from them, obviously. But to one of the six or so other extra-terrestrial shamanic prophets, there will be numerous rays of light and colour and emanations and that coming off of me now, like nobody's business.

Wallace says I have a kind of purple aura that starts glowing round me at meal times but that's either his imagination or he's just trying to knuckle in. Seeing as the only way Wallace could spot this would be if *he* was a Chosen One too, which is impossible, obviously, seeing as the Sentinels of the Universe, with all due respect, would hardly make *Wallace* an extra-terrestrial shamanic prophet – endowed with the massive responsibility of leading the entire human race out of the bottomless pit into the golden dawn of the eternal sunlight. Not unless they wanted their heads examining, anyway!

Now, of course, he's saying he has a purple light around *him* that *I* can't see – which is absurd, obviously. Wallace has NO LIGHT AROUND HIM AND THAT IS AN END TO IT! Obviously, as I was told by the Sentinels, I am not here to judge human nature, but to lead it into a New

Age of Light and Inner Peace free of all conflict and duality, but Wallace would do well to remember that it was *me* who had the vision and not him. Besides which, they'd hardly have two Shamans in the *same house*, would they? Seeing as there's only half a dozen in the whole world. If he'd been made a Shaman, they'd have put him in China or somewhere.
And the best place for him, probably, if you ask me.

THINGS TO DO:

1. Upon awakening, try examining your dreams for tell-tale signs of possible extra-terrestrial visitation. Whilst the Chosen Ones themselves have all been chosen, obviously, I should imagine that they will almost certainly be interviewing for junior Sentinels, assistant Chosen Ones, etc. to help with filing and so forth.
2. Learn some simple shamanic techniques for use in the home (*See* illustrations below).

Fig. i *Swallowing hot embers*

Fig. ii *Self-stabbing without wounding*

Fig. iii *Predicting the movement of game*

CHAPTER LXVI

THE PRESENT DAY

'So what does the future hold?'

(Desmond Olivier Dingle)

SO where will this little cosmic wanderer called earth go now? Do we have a future? Who can tell? All these crucial questions are ones that no–one can answer. And unfortunately, much as I would like to, neither can I. Seeing as, at the time of writing, I am slightly overdue with the deadline to deliver the text to Methuen's, which you have just read, hopefully. Otherwise I would of course be fascinated to delve into such speculations. And so it is that we must leave this planet, whereon we are, where she is today, and look forward proudly to where she will be tomorrow.

A Personal Note

I would just like to say, before closing, that, in my humble opinion, it will now be reasonably obvious to anyone with a modicum of literary insight that – albeit this is my first published *oeuvre* – I am clearly an author of potentially massive proportions.

For this reason, I am currently planning a number of works as major follow-ups. In particular, my first novel, which, owing to prior commitments, I have not yet had the opportunity of starting, but which is very clearly mapped out in my mind, so to speak, and I will be entering for the Christopher Booker Prize in 1988. Tentatively called *The Sleuth, the Egyptian and the Actress*, it concerns a millionaire playboy detective who has to rescue a beautiful Shakespearian actress, absconded from her Stratford-on-Avon cottage by Rasputin's grandson and taken to his fortress in the Himalayas, or possibly Bali. To assist him in this task, the millionaire detective is aided by a re-incarnated pharaoh, who thus becomes a close and personal friend for life. Obviously it is still in a somewhat rudimentary form and I haven't as yet tied together all the strands of the allegorical infra-structure that interweaves the uncompromisingly adult central plot. But the final version should, I hope, be something like a fascinating blend of Desmond Bagley and Iris Murdoch.

Naturally, Methuen's and myself will be discussing publication of this, my first novel, in the very near future. However, I would just like to say that it is not necessarily absolutely *essential* that Methuen's should be the publishers. In fact – to be perfectly candid – it is my belief that Methuen's are probably a little bit over the hill for modern novels, as it happens. Not Sir Geoffrey, obviously, who is one of the finest men who ever lived. But clearly he can't soldier on indefinitely.

And once he goes, who knows what could happen? Besides which, the offices are very pokey and tea and coffee facilities *virtually non-existent*. In other words, and loyal as I am to Methuen's, they have in my opinion, basically gone to the dogs.

In Conclusion

Finally and in conclusion, as this mighty work draws to its historic close, I would just like to briefly refer to the footnote at the foot of page 155, in which I state that Methuen's are more prestigious than other publishers. *What I meant*, of course, was that Methuen's *go round saying* they are more prestigious than other publishers, which is a different kettle of fish altogether, obviously! And another example of a rather arrogant attitude that I have begun to observe more and more at Methuen's, to be honest. I think I need say no more.

In fact, it is my belief that such publishers as Penguin's, Chatto and Windus, Thames and Hudson and Patricia Routledge and Paul, while perhaps not having the years of expertise that Methuen's have behind them, do have a massive amount to offer contemporary novelists such as myself, dealing as we do with the harshly truthful yet deeply poetic realities of today. For this reason, therefore, I would be extremely interested in starting the financial ball rolling, so to speak, with respect to commissioning the above novel – my first major work of fiction. Or if this didn't appeal, to have a go at any other ideas they might have knocking around.

In other words, I am 'in the market', as it were, should any interest be forthcoming and have certainly not closed my doors to anyone else at this juncture. In fact, if any publisher were able to make an immediate cash advance, either in the form of a lump sum or the disbursement of certain bills or mortgages (or both), then I can safely say this offer would be very favourably examined by my financial advisers and given a profoundly fair hearing indeed. In fact I have always believed that it's very very important not to close doors anywhere, as it were. Particularly today, obviously.

Should any such funding be forthcoming, please address all correspondence (UNDER PLAIN COVER) to Desmond Olivier Dingle, c/o

THE PRESENT DAY

Authors' Suite, Methuen Books, New Fetter Lane, London E.C.1, Great Britain.

THINGS TO DO:

1. Discover your family tree. You may well be surprised at your illustrious ancestry (as I was, for example, to discover not only direct lines to Henry V and Edward the Professor, but also fascinating connections with Jane Austen, Hereward the Wake, Bob Geldof and Mozart. To mention but a few.). However, don't get *too* excited. Some families have only recently started, such as Wallace's, for example, which only began in 1953.

2. Give this book to a friend as a stylish and lasting gift that will be treasured for years to come (including a *free leaflet* describing a host of exciting ways to display it in the home). Just simply fill in the form below and return to Marketing Dept, Methuen Books, New Fetter Lane Ltd., London E.C.1, Great Britain.

YES PLEASE, METHUEN'S!

RUSH a copy of ALL THE WORLD'S A GLOBE to

....

address ....

....

....

as a surprise gift that I believe he/she★ and their children will treasure for the rest of their lives.

TOGETHER WITH a free *two-colour* leaflet describing a host of exciting ways to display it in the home.

CHOOSE YOUR BINDING AND TICK WHERE APPLICABLE:

The 'Classic': £8.95 (plus p+p)

The 'Renaissance' (including simulated Medieval Bookmark): £40.00 (plus p+p)

The 'Babylonian' (including Medieval Bookmark, replica Viking Bookstand and Author's signature. Limited to 500 only): £1000.00 (p+p extra)
★ *Delete where necessary.*

CHAPTER LXVII
POSTLUDE

'The thing that gave me most joy was this. I was walking across the reception rooms when I heard a voice crying "Cuckoo". It was Princess Margaret.'

(Sir Peter Hall – *The Secret Diary of Peter Hall*)

AND so we spin on in space, going who knows where.

THINGS TO DO:

1. Précis this chapter in your own words.